Field Guide to
COOKIES

How to Identify and Bake Virtually Every Cookie Imaginable

By Anita Chu

Consultation by Caroline Romanski

QUIRK BOOKS

PHILADELPHIA

Copyright © 2008 by Quirk Productions, Inc.

Library of Congress Cataloging in Publication Number: 2008926881

ISBN: 978-1-59474-283-5

Printed in Singapore

Typeset in Adobe, Garamond, Franklin Gothic, and Impact

Designed by Michael Rogalski
Photography by Steve Legato
Iconography by Karen Onorato
Edited by Margaret McGuire and Erin Slonaker

Distributed in North America by Chronicle Books
680 Second Street
San Francisco, CA 94107

10 9 8 7 6 5 4 3 2

Quirk Books
215 Church Street
Philadelphia, PA 19106
www.quirkbooks.com

Contents

BAR COOKIES

MOLDED COOKIES

ROLLED COOKIES

INTRODUCTION

Few things bring as much simple joy as a freshly baked cookie. Some may think cakes and tarts too time-consuming to make, or consider other fancy desserts too filling or complicated, but hardly anyone refuses a cookie. Cookies are easy to make, transport, and consume—the ultimate comfort food. These small, sweet confections carry associations of childhood, of watching mom stirring a batch of dough, or of eating a warm plate of cookies with a glass of milk. They are linked to many holidays and festivals around the world, where celebrations are capped with a tray of beautifully decorated cookies.

The word *cookie* comes from the Dutch word *koekje*, the diminutive form of *koek*, which means "cake." But cookies are so much more than little cakes—for centuries, they have been baked as individually portioned sweet treats for special occasions, from religious holidays to birthdays. The first cookie-style sugar cakes were baked in 7th-century Persia, which was one of the first regions to cultivate sugar. Cookies can be found in an astonishing variety of forms around the world, but all cookies have several characteristics in common: They are individually portioned; they are firm and compact enough to be eaten by hand; and, with a few exceptions, they are flat compared with muffins or other pastries. There are a few basic cookie categories: **drop cookie** dough is dropped in spoonfuls, piped from a pastry bag, or dispensed with a cookie press; **bar cookie** dough is spread into a pan and baked, then cut into individual pieces; **molded cookie** dough is pressed into a mold with an imprinted design, or otherwise shaped before it is baked; **rolled cookie** dough is rolled out and cut into shapes with a cookie cutter. Elaborately decorated cookies are often rolled, since it creates a smooth surface perfect for decorating. Almost any cookie can be turned into a sandwich cookie by combining two cookies with a sweet filling, such as jam, chocolate, or ice cream.

This book will help you identify many of the most popular cookies around the world, discover what makes each one special, and recreate them in your home kitchen. You will find that even though many cookies appear different on the outside, they can be made with similar techniques. You'll also learn about some basic tools and techniques that will ensure bakery-perfect cookies every time, as well as simple ways to vary cookie recipes to further increase your repertoire. With this guide, you'll never have to worry about an empty cookie jar at your house.

NOTES ON THE PERFECT COOKIE

Alterations and substitutions. The first time you try a recipe, follow it as written without alterations. Once you have an understanding of how the recipe works, play around with it to suit your tastes.

Baking time. In a just a few minutes, cookies can go from golden to burned. Check the cookies a few minutes before they are supposed to be done, but don't open the oven too wide; that lowers the temperature inside the oven and it will take longer for the cookies to bake.

Cookie size. Keep your cookies as close to the same size as possible so they will bake evenly.

Creaming. During the process of creaming, sugar cuts little air pockets into butter, giving cookies a fine, fluffy texture. For this reason, it's important to use softened, room temperature butter. Beat butter first to soften it before adding sugar. Then cream the two ingredients for several minutes until the mixture lightens in color from yellow to almost white, and it becomes smooth and fluffy.

Folding. When folding ingredients into a batter, the goal is to incorporate them without deflating the mixture. Place lighter, drier ingredients on top of the wet batter and fold them in gently with a large rubber spatula, starting at the back edge of the bowl. Scoop down and toward you, bringing batter from the bottom up and over the ingredients on top. Rotate the bowl a quarter turn and repeat this motion.

Ingredient temperature. The temperature of ingredients is very important to their performance in a recipe. Be sure to note if a recipe calls for any of them to be cold or room temperature. Dry ingredients such as flour and sugar should always be at room temperature; if you have been storing them in the refrigerator take them out an hour or so before baking. Eggs should also be used at room temperature; if you've forgotten to take them out beforehand, warm them in a bowl filled with lukewarm water. If the recipe calls for cold butter, take it out right before you start the recipe, and use it quickly to prevent it from warming up and melting. If the butter is to be "softened" or "room temperature," this means within a range of 65 to 70°F. It should be soft enough to yield slightly beneath your finger, but not oily or melting. Take butter out of the refrigerator an hour before baking. If you slice a stick of butter into pieces, it will soften much faster.

Measuring. Careful and precise measuring of ingredients will help your cookies come out perfect every time. When measuring flour, spoon the flour into the measuring cup until it mounds over the top, then use an offset spatula or the edge of a knife to level it off. Do not use the measuring cup to scoop flour or shake the cup as you spoon flour in; it compacts too much flour into the cup. Measure flour first before sifting it. Use the same method of spooning in and leveling off when measuring granulated and confectioners' sugar. When measuring brown sugar, lightly pack it into the measuring cup, then level the top off. When measuring liquids, use a glass measuring cup and check the liquid at eye level. The surface of the liquid will usually bow slightly in the middle; check the lowest point of the liquid, not the highest.

Melting chocolate. The best way to melt chocolate is on the stove in a double boiler or a metal or glass bowl set over a pot of simmering water. Be sure that the water in the pot doesn't touch the bottom of the bowl and that the bowl fits into the pot so steam won't escape. If any moisture gets into melting chocolate, it will become chunky and unusable. The key to melting chocolate is gentle, low heat. If chocolate burns, it becomes thick and clumpy. Take the bowl off the stove when the chocolate seems almost fully melted and then stir the mixture to melt the last small bits. Chocolate can be melted in the microwave, but proceed with caution. Microwave uncovered and in 30-second increments, stirring well after each session.

Mixing. A stand mixer is the easiest way to quickly and thoroughly mix ingredients. Don't mix more than necessary—the gluten in the flour will overdevelop, leading to tough cookies. When adding dry ingredients to dough, keep the speed on low to medium and mix only until the dry ingredients have been incorporated. Hand mixers take longer to bring dough together, so move the mixer around the bowl to thoroughly mix all parts of the dough. Whether using a stand mixer or hand mixer, scrape down the sides and bottom of the bowl at least once to catch any unincorporated bits. It is also possible for the strong of arm to make cookies by hand. All you need is a large bowl for the ingredients and a wooden spoon. Drop and bar cookies are the easiest to make by hand.

Oven temperature. Check your oven's temperature with an oven thermometer. If you notice your oven tends to be hot or cold, adjust the baking time accordingly. All ovens have hot spots, causing cookies in one corner to bake faster than the rest. Rotate cookie sheets halfway through baking for evenly baked cookies.

Piping. When filling a pastry bag, hold it in one hand and roll the top down halfway over your hand to form a secure "cup" for the batter. Or place the bag tip down into a tall glass and roll the top of the bag down around the glass. Use a rubber spatula to fill the bag half full. Then roll up the top of the bag and twist it shut, pushing the batter down to the tip. With one hand, hold the bag near the top where it is twisted shut, and apply pressure from there. Place your other hand lightly on the bag near the tip to guide it. Apply even, steady pressure and release the pressure before pulling the bag away to get a clean break instead of trailing batter.

Refrigeration. When you store cookie dough in the refrigerator, prevent it from drying out or absorbing odors by wrapping it in two layers of plastic wrap, or packing it into a container and covering the top with plastic wrap underneath the lid. Freeze cookie dough in balls arranged on a baking sheet wrapped in plastic or in freezer bags.

Whipping egg whites. The purpose of whipping egg whites is to create as much volume as possible by whipping air into the whites. Air trapped in egg whites expands through baking to create a light, fluffy texture in the finished cookie. For best results, whip egg whites at room temperature. If you can plan even further ahead, separate the eggs the night before and store the whites in the refrigerator overnight, taking them out an hour before whipping. The fat in egg yolks prevents egg whites from whipping up well, so make sure no yolk is mixed in. Egg whites whip best in a copper bowl, because the proteins in the whites react with the copper; however, a stand mixer with the whisk attachment is fine. Be sure the bowl and the whisk are clean and free of grease—it inhibits the whipping process. If you are whipping to soft peaks, the whites should pull up when you pull the whisk out, with the peaks falling back over. If you are whipping to stiff peaks, whip a little longer until the peaks stay straight when you pull the whisk out. Be careful when you are whipping to stiff peaks; if the egg whites become curdled with a broken, foamy appearance, they have been overwhipped, and you must start over. Stop when the whites seem almost perfect, then finish by hand.

NOTES ON BAKING TOOLS

Having the right tools to make cookies will result in better cookies and make the baking process more enjoyable.

Baking pans. The most common sizes are 8 by 8, 9 by 9, and 9 by 13 inches and at least 2 inches deep. Baking pans should be made of glass, pyrex, or metal, preferably aluminum. Pans with dark, nonstick surfaces may cause cookies to bake faster and brown on the outside before the insides have finished baking.

Cookie cutters. Choose sturdy metal cutters that will hold their shape. Dip cookie cutters into sugar or flour to prevent them from sticking to softer doughs.

Cookie scoop. The most useful types of scoops—also known as *dishers*—have a narrow arm that sweeps around the curve of the scoop to quickly release the dough. Scoops come in two forms: spring-loaded squeeze handles or a solid one-piece handle with a lever release. A tablespoon can substitute for a cookie scoop in a pinch.

Cookie sheets. Most cookie sheets have one to three edges that are turned up for easier handling—fewer edges allows for better air circulation, baking cookies faster and more evenly. Choose heavy, solid sheets; flimsy sheets warp in a hot oven. Thick sheets of shiny aluminum are best. Nonstick sheets may cause the cookie exteriors to darken too much before the cookies have finished baking. Insulated cookie sheets may lengthen the baking time (recipes note when they are not appropriate to use). Jelly roll pans, or *sheet pans*, are sized slightly differently from cookie sheets and rimmed on all four sides.

Cooking spray. Use a flavorless vegetable oil–based spray to avoid adding unwanted flavors. Alternatively, grease sheets with butter or use silicone baking mats or parchment paper.

Food processor. A food procesor is invaluable for grinding nuts and combining ingredients together. Some recipes require nuts to be ground to a fineness that cannot be achieved by hand chopping. If you don't have access to a food processor, ground nuts can be found at the supermarket.

Knives. There are three essentials in the pastry kitchen: a small paring knife; a 6- to 8-inch chef's knife; and a serrated bread knife.

Measuring cups. For dry measuring cups, a graduated set in stainless steel is best. Use a liquid measuring cup made of heavy glass with a 2-cup capacity and both standard and metric measurements.

Measuring spoons. Stainless steel measuring spoons are long-lasting and precise. Spoons with a narrow, long shape fit easily into small spice jars.

Mixers. Most of the recipes in this book can be made with a hand mixer, a stand mixer, or by hand. All recipes note where a stand mixer is absolutely required.

Parchment paper is coated with silicone so cookies come right off the nonstick surface without cooking spray or butter. Parchment paper is not the same as wax paper; wax paper could melt and burn in the oven.

Pastry bag. A 14-inch pastry bag is standard. Bags are made of disposable plastic, canvas coated with plastic on the inside, or poly/nylon material. Wash immediately after use in hot soapy water and hang to dry (the bag lining may absorb grease or odors if it is improperly cleaned). A variety of pastry tips are available for decorating, but for piping dough you need only a basic round tip.

Rolling pin. Most bakers are familiar with rolling pins that have handles, but give the French-style solid pins a try: They allow better control over the dough. Wood rolling pins work well. Silicone rolling pins may be more effective at preventing dough from sticking but are not necessary.

The weight of marble rolling pins is well balanced, and they can be chilled—helpful when dough is sticky or a recipe calls for chilled butter.

Ruler. A metal ruler comes in handy for measuring dough and cutting bar cookies evenly.

Sifter. Sifters remove lumps from dry ingredients like confectioners' sugar and cornstarch. A sieve will work equally well; fine mesh is best.

Silicone baking mats. Cookies come right off silicone baking mats; there's no need for butter or cooking spray, and the mats are reusable.

Spatulas. Use rubber spatulas to fold mix-ins into cookie batter or scrape dough out of a bowl. Wide metal spatulas are indispensable for removing cookies from sheets. An offset spatula has a long, thin metal blade bent slightly below the handle (hence its name); use it to level dry ingredients or spread icing smoothly.

Whisk. Use a whisk rather than a spoon to combine dry ingredients thoroughly and eliminates clumps. Whisks are also good for beating eggs and stirring custards to prevent lumps from forming. An 8-inch (medium-sized) whisk is most useful. Balloon whisks are wider, and thus handy for whipping egg whites and cream.

Wire racks. Cooling racks are essential for protecting your tables from hot pans and for cooling cookies properly by letting air circulate around them.

NOTES ON BAKING INGREDIENTS

Most cookies in this book can be made without any special or expensive ingredients—that's one of the joys of cookies. It helps to have a little knowledge about some of the most common cookie ingredients to ensure the best results.

Baking powder combines baking soda with acid and cornstarch, which absorb moisture and prevent it from activating before being used. Baking powder eliminates the need to specifically calibrate acidic ingredients in recipes. Almost all baking powders available today are double action: they work once during the mixing process and again in the oven. Baking powder loses its potency after 9 months. Check to see if your baking powder is still active by dropping a teaspoon into a cup of water—it should bubble.

Baking soda forms carbon dioxide by reacting with acidic ingredients: chocolate, buttermilk, sour cream, molasses, lemon juice, or cream of tartar. If you omit acidic ingredients in a baking soda recipe, add an equal amount of another acid or use baking powder instead. Keep baking soda in a cool, dark, airtight place; moisture can cause baking soda to activate. Baking soda lasts 6 to 9 months; to test whether it is still active, drop a teaspoon into vinegar—it should bubble.

Brown sugar contains more moisture than granulated sugar, making cookies softer and chewier. It is simply granulated sugar with molasses added. Dark brown sugar contains more molasses than light brown sugar and has a darker, stronger flavor. When measured, brown sugar should be lightly packed down into the measuring cup. It dries out very quickly when exposed to air, so keep it tightly covered.

Butter used for cookie baking must be fresh: It should smell sweet. Butter should be kept well wrapped in the refrigerator, as it can pick up odors very easily. Butter used in baking should always be unsalted. Stick margarine can be substituted for stick butter, but margarine does not impart the same richness of flavor, and some formulations of margarine may perform differently. Avoid margarine spreads or other synthetic butter substitutes.

Chocolate. Most recipes using chocolate work best with a dark chocolate with 65–70 percent cacao content. Most sweetened and bittersweet chocolates fall within this range. Unsweetened chocolates are too bitter and don't have enough fat. Do not substitute milk chocolate for dark chocolate, as the milk solids will affect the recipe's result.

Chocolate chips. Contrary to intuition, chocolate chips are entirely different from bar chocolate. Chips have been specially formulated to keep their shape during baking, so they will not melt the same way; *never substitute chocolate chips for chocolate*. However, chopped pieces of chocolate can be substituted for chocolate chips for a flavorful, sophisticated touch.

Confectioners' sugar. This is granulated sugar combined with cornstarch and ground to ten times the fineness of standard granulated sugar. It is also called *powdered sugar*, *confectionary sugar*, or *10X sugar*. Confectioners' sugar tends to clump; sift for best results.

Cream. Whipping cream (or *whipped cream*) is made with varying percentages of butterfat. Use a whipping cream with at least 36 percent butterfat; in North America this is called *heavy cream*. In the United Kingdom, double cream—about 48 percent butterfat—is used.

Eggs. All the recipes in this book call for large eggs, the standard size for baking. The fresher eggs are, the better they perform. Recipes that use whipped egg whites are the exception to the fresh-egg rule: *Egg whites that have aged for a few days will attain the most volume when whipped.* Store eggs in the back of the refrigerator where it is coldest. Keep eggs in their original container, as it prevents them from absorbing odors. Separated eggs can be refrigerated in airtight containers for 3–4 days. Eggs should be used at room temperature; if you've forgotten to take them out beforehand, warm them in a bowl of lukewarm water.

Flour. Although there's a dazzling array of flours available in the market today, the most common flour for baking is still all-purpose flour (A.P. flour). Unbleached all-purpose flour works just as well, although it may affect the color of the cookies. Cake flour has less gluten content than all-purpose flour, which give delicate cookies a light, tender texture. Store all flour in a cool, dry place away from light and heat.

Milk. Whole milk is best for baking. Avoid substituting lower-fat milk: the difference in fat content changes how the cookies turn out. Without the fat, cookies can be flat, hard, less flavorful, and more likely to burn in the oven.

Mix-ins. From nuts to chocolate chips, mix-ins are extras that can be added to cookie dough without affecting the chemical reactions that occur during baking.

Nuts. Nuts go rancid quickly, so take care to choose fresh nuts and store them in the refrigerator for a few months or in the freezer for up to a year.

Phyllo dough (puff pastry). Making phyllo or puff pastry at home can be a time-consuming process, but packages of phyllo sheets and puff pastry can be found in the frozen foods section of most markets. When using a puff pastry, pick one made with all butter and as few preservatives as possible for the best flavor and performance.

Sugar. Sugar caramelizes during baking, giving cookies a golden brown color. When creamed with butter, sugar creates little air pockets in the butter; this aeration creates a fluffy, tender cookie texture—so don't use superfine sugar in place of regular granulated.

Vanilla. Be sure to use pure vanilla extract; imitation vanilla extract is a poor substitute for the real thing.

Drop Cookies

1. **AMARETTI (ITALIAN MACAROONS)**

General
Description:

Amaretti are a modern Italian version of the original macaroons invented centuries ago in Italy. They are small, round, pale golden cookies, with a crisp outer shell and a soft, lightly chewy center. *Amaro* means "bitter" in Italian, so *amaretti* means "little bitter ones." These small cookies are often a component of Italian desserts; crushed amaretti are used as layers in tortes and frozen desserts.

History:

Macaroons originated in Italy in the 14th or 15th century, most likely in monasteries. They were called *maccarone*, a word that originally referred to any cookie that was made from egg whites mixed with nuts, and myriad variations across Italy call for different nuts. *Amaretti* originally referred to a particular variation in the mid-1600s created by the pastry chef at the court of Savoy, Francesco Moriondo, but now *amaretti* is used to describe all Italian macaroons.

Serving
Suggestions:

These versatile cookies can be served as a simple treat, or they can embellish other desserts, from tortes to gelato. Amaretti go very well with ice creams and mousses, served alongside them or crushed and sprinkled over the top. Layer crushed amaretti with ice cream and fruit to make a simple and elegant parfait. Amaretti have accompanied fruit, sweet dessert wines, and coffee for centuries. Elegantly wrapped amaretti are a common guest at Italian weddings.

Baking Notes: Grind the almonds to as fine a consistency as possible —sift out any large bits. Grinding them with the sugar prevents the nuts from being pulverized into a paste, as the sugar absorbs some of the nut oils.

Recipe: **1 cup blanched almonds**
2/3 cup sugar
5 teaspoons all-purpose flour
1/8 teaspoon salt
2 egg whites
3/4 teaspoon almond extract
Confectioners' sugar for sifting

1. **Preheat oven to 300°F. Line several cookie sheets with parchment paper or silicone baking mats.**

2. **Using a food processor, grind almonds, sugar, flour, and salt to a fine meal.**

3. **Place ground almond mixture in a large bowl, and add the egg whites and almond extract. Mix with a rubber spatula until combined.**

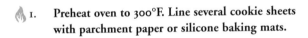

4. **Drop dough by teaspoonfuls onto sheets about 1½**

**inches apart. If desired, sift confectioners' sugar
over cookies before baking. Bake 18 to 20 minutes,
rotating cookie sheets halfway through; when
amaretti are done baking, the edges will be golden
brown. Cool sheets on wire racks for 5 minutes
before transferring cookies directly onto wire racks
with a metal spatula to finish cooling.**

Yield: About 3 dozen cookies

Storage: Store in an airtight container for five to seven days.
 Amaretti get chewier and crunchier as they age, and
their almond flavor intensifies (perfect with a cup of
espresso).

Variation: Top amaretti with a traditional Italian treat: *confetti*,
which are sugar-coated almonds.

2a–b. **AMISH PUFF COOKIES**

General *Amish puff cookies are based on old German baking*
Description: *techniques, but they have become a uniquely American
tradition.* These light, fluffy cookies puff up in the
oven before settling down to a crinkly appearance.
Coated in sugar, they are similar to **snickerdoodles**,
another classic American cookie.

History: This classic Amish recipe has spread across America far beyond the small Amish communities that popularized it. It is not uncommon to find Amish sellers at farmers' markets, selling quickbreads, produce, and a variety of other foods.

Serving
Suggestions:

Amish puff cookies are suitable for a variety of occasions, from barbecues and picnics to Thanksgiving feasts. In the fall and winter, they are great with a glass of cider.

Baking Notes:

These cookies will puff up when baking and then settle down, giving them a crinkly appearance.

Recipe:

1½ cups all-purpose flour
½ teaspoon baking powder
½ teaspoon baking soda
½ teaspoon cream of tartar
¼ teaspoon salt
½ cup softened unsalted butter
½ cup light brown sugar
¼ cup sugar
1 egg
¼ cup sugar
4 teaspoons ground cinnamon

 1. **Sift the flour, baking powder, baking soda, cream of tartar, and salt into a bowl and set aside.**

 2. **In a stand mixer, cream butter and sugars on medium**

speed for several minutes until light and fluffy. Add
the egg and mix until combined.

3. Add the flour mixture, and mix on low speed just
until combined.

4. Cover dough and refrigerate for 30 minutes.

5. For the cinnamon sugar: Combine sugar and cinnamon in a bowl.

6. Preheat the oven to 375°F. Line several cookie sheets
with parchment paper.

7. Roll tablespoon-sized balls of dough in the cinnamon
sugar and place on cookie sheets about 3 inches apart.

8. Bake for 8 to 10 minutes, rotating sheets halfway
through, until golden brown. Cool cookie sheets on
wire racks.

Yield: About 2 dozen cookies

Storage: Store in an airtight container for up to 1 week.

Variation: ***Chocolate Chip Puff Cookies***
Fold 1 cup of chocolate chips into the dough after
completing step 4 and omit the cinnamon-sugar

coating in steps 5 and 7.

ANZAC BISCUITS

General
Description:

Few cookies are as deeply entrenched in the culture and history of a nation as these fiber-filled, travel-hardy oatmeal biscuits. Affectionately known as *bikkies*, ANZAC biscuits are national favorites in Australia and New Zealand, where they can be found in supermarkets, "biscuit shops," and restaurants year-round but are baked in great numbers on ANZAC Day, April 25. ANZAC biscuits may have evolved from Scottish rolled oat cake recipes or **rock cakes**.

History:

During World War I, two military divisions of Australian and New Zealand soldiers joined to create the Australian and New Zealand Army Corps, ANZAC. They were sent to Egypt for training, and they brought with them simple, travel-worthy oatmeal cookies. The courageous ANZAC forces became renowned for their valiant service at Gallipoli, Turkey. In 1920, April 25 was declared ANZAC day, celebrated in Australia, New Zealand, Cooks Islands, Tonga, and Samoa. It has since been expanded to a memorial day that honors all who served in World Wars I, II, Korea, and Vietnam. Tins of ANZAC biscuits are often sold as fundraising for veterans, and they are used as Australian military rations to this day.

Serving
Suggestions:

These biscuits make a durable, nutritious meal for hikers, travelers, and Australian bushwalkers. ANZAC biscuits are commonly dunked in tea or dark coffee.

Baking Notes:

These tasty biscuits are unusual for their lack of (perishable) eggs as well as their long baking time. Golden syrup, rendered from inverted sugar, is widely popular throughout the world, but less so in America. Although it can be found in the United States, it can be replaced with treacle, light corn syrup, or maple syrup.

Recipe:

1 cup rolled oats
1 cup all-purpose flour
¹/₂ cup sugar
¹/₂ cup dark brown sugar
³/₄ cup sweetened flaked coconut (optional)
2 tablespoons golden syrup
¹/₂ cup softened unsalted butter
³/₄ teaspoon baking soda

 1. **Preheat oven to 325°F. Grease several cookie sheets.**

 2. **Combine oats, flour, sugars, and coconut in a medium bowl and set aside.**

3. In a small saucepan, melt syrup and butter over medium-high heat, stirring with a wooden spoon. Simultaneously boil 2–3 tablespoons of water.

 4. In a small bowl, combine baking soda with 2 tablespoons boiling water; add the syrup and butter mixture, and stir to combine.

 5. Mix syrup mixture into the flour mixture until evenly combined.

 6. Drop tablespoon-sized balls of dough onto sheets about 2 inches apart. Bake for 18–20 minutes, rotating cookie sheets halfway through; finished ANZAC biscuits are a honeyed, golden color. Cool cookie sheets on wire racks.

Yield: About 2 dozen biscuits

Storage: Hardy ANZAC biscuits are perhaps the most non-perishable baked good; they are engineered for a long shelf-life. Sealed airtight at room temperature, they keep for more than 3 weeks; they can be frozen for more than 3 months. They are traditionally stored in reusable metal tins.

Variation: ***Trail Mix ANZAC Biscuits***
 Add up to 1 cup of your favorite mix-ins to the dough in step 5—try sesame seeds, peanuts, dried

berries, or chocolate chips.

4. **BANANA CHOCOLATE CHIP COOKIES**

General
Description:

These soft, chewy cookies combine the taste and aroma of banana bread with the full flavor of dark chocolate chips. Banana chocolate chip cookies transform banana bread into a dessert, following a common principle by which many home bakers adapt a standard recipe into a bite-sized cookie: If it's sweet, make it sweeter.

History:

The 1900s marked a proliferation of novel cookie recipes and quick breads (such as banana bread) as a great variety of ingredients became increasingly available to general consumers. Quick breads don't call for yeast; they rely instead upon chemical leaveners (see **baking powder** and **baking soda**, page 10). Although the earliest date of banana bread is unknown, Pillsbury published a recipe in 1933.

Serving
Suggestions:

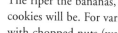

Serve banana chocolate chip cookies with a cold glass of milk, vanilla ice cream, or a decadent banana split.

Baking Notes:

The riper the bananas, the more flavorful these cookies will be. For variety, substitute chocolate chips with chopped nuts (walnuts, pecans, macadamias or cashews), or a use combination of mix-ins such as $^1/_2$ cup dark chocolate chips, $^1/_2$ cup chopped nuts, and $^1/_4$ cup shredded sweetened coconut.

Recipe: **1$^1/_2$ cups all-purpose flour**
1$^3/_4$ cups rolled old-fashioned oats
$^1/_2$ teaspoon baking soda
$^1/_2$ teaspoon ground cinnamon
1 teaspoon salt
$^3/_4$ cup softened unsalted butter
1 cup sugar
1 egg
$^1/_2$ teaspoon vanilla extract
1 cup mashed ripe bananas
1 cup (6 oz) chocolate chips

 1. Preheat the oven to 375°F. Line several cookie sheets with parchment paper or silicone baking mats.

 2. Sift the flour, oats, baking soda, cinnamon, and salt into a bowl and set aside.

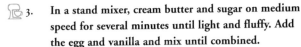 3. In a stand mixer, cream butter and sugar on medium speed for several minutes until light and fluffy. Add the egg and vanilla and mix until combined.

4. Add half of the flour mixture, and mix on low speed just until combined; add the bananas and mix to combine. Add the rest of the flour mixture and mix

until combined. Mix in chocolate chips.

 5. Drop tablespoon-sized balls of dough onto cookie sheets about 2 inches apart.

 6. Bake for 12 to 14 minutes, rotating sheets halfway through. Cool sheets on wire racks for a few minutes before transferring cookies directly onto wire racks with a spatula to finish cooling.

Yield: About 3¹/2 dozen cookies

Storage: Store in a single layer in an airtight container for up to 5 days. These cookies are quite soft, so don't stack them.

5. **BLACK AND WHITE COOKIES**

General
Description: *Black and white cookies are soft, cakelike, lightly lemony cookies with distinctive icing.* The frosted top—one half chocolate icing, the other half vanilla icing—is the distinguishing characteristic. The typical black and white cookie is oversized at 3¹/2 to 4 inches in diameter. The cakey texture of the cookie has given it the reputation of a "cookie made from cake batter," but most recipes for the cookie do not have the same ingredient proportions as that of a cake. The icing is sometimes a creamy fondant, or sometimes a thin-

ner, harder consistency, but it is always made with confectioners' sugar.

New York City is strongly affiliated with the black and white cookie, and many residents consider the black and white cookie an unofficial symbol of the city. In other parts of America, the cookie is sometimes called a half-moon cookie, and in Germany a version of the cookie is called the *Amerikaner* ("American").

History:

Black and white cookies first appeared in New York during the 1940s. Hemstrought's Bakery in Utica claims the honor of originating the cookie; however, black and white cookies quickly became ubiquitous among bakeries and delis in New York City.

Serving Suggestions:

If you don't want the traditional mild lemon flavor, omit it and use only vanilla extract. Frost the cookies entirely in chocolate or white icing for a nontraditional look.

Baking Notes:

Avoid overbaking; the hallmark of this cookie is its soft, moist, cakelike texture. The easiest way to frost the cookies quickly and smoothly is with a small offset spatula. To avoid making a mess, place the finished, cooled cookies on a wire rack over a piece of wax paper to catch the drips. To make a straight line down the center, use the spatula to lightly mark a dividing line on the cookie before you frost it.

Recipe: **4 cups cake flour**
           ¹/₂ teaspoon baking powder
           ¹/₂ teaspoon salt
           1 cup softened unsalted butter
           1³/₄ cups sugar
           ¹/₂ teaspoon vanilla extract
           ¹/₂ teaspoon lemon extract
           4 egg whites
           ³/₄ cups milk

           Icing:
           6 cups confectioners' sugar
           9 tablespoons milk (more as needed)
           1¹/₂ teaspoons vanilla extract
           4 tablespoons cocoa powder

 1.   Preheat oven to 375°F. Grease several cookie sheets.

 2.   Sift flour, baking powder, and salt into a medium bowl and set aside.

 3.   In a stand mixer, beat butter on medium to medium-high speed for several minutes until smooth.

 4.   With the mixer on low speed, add sugar in a slow stream. Cream butter and sugar on medium-high speed for several minutes until very light (almost white) and fluffy.

5. Add both extracts, then add egg whites one at a time; mix to combine between each addition.

6. Add the flour mixture and milk in alternating additions, 3 additions of each starting with the flour mixture. Mix just until combined.

7. Drop 1/4 cup–sized scoops of dough onto cookie sheets, about 5 inches apart.

8. Wet a small offset spatula or butter knife with water. Spread each cookie ball into a 3-inch round, creating as smooth a surface as possible. Continue to wet spatula as needed to smooth each top.

9. Bake for 8 to 10 minutes, rotating sheets halfway through, until edges just begin to turn golden. Cool sheets on wire racks.

10. For the icing: Mix the confectioners' sugar, milk, and vanilla in a bowl until smooth. Transfer half of the icing to another bowl and add cocoa powder. Be sure to mix until cocoa powder lumps have disappeared. Using a small offset spatula, spread the chocolate icing on half of the cookie. Follow with the vanilla icing on the other half.

11. Allow the iced cookies to set for 30 minutes on wire racks, then remove them with a metal spatula.

Yield:	About 2 dozen cookies

Storage:	Store cookies in an airtight container, layered between wax paper, for up to 3 days.

---

6. **BRANDY SNAPS**

General
Description:
Resembling works of blown glass, brandy snaps are filled with a light whipped cream and scented with brandy and a touch of chocolate. Strong flavors of sweet brandy and ginger are rolled into a thin, delicate cookie shell around whipped cream or another filling.

History:
Brandy snaps originated in the United Kingdom, where they have been popular for more than a century. In Victorian England, they were common at fairs and bazaars, served beside such diverse items as tripe, oysters, and ginger bread. Nowadays they are commonly found filled with cream in old-fashioned country pubs, stuck in a sticky toffee pudding for tea, or filled with strawberry ice cream for a summer evening dessert.

Serving
Suggestions:
The playful balance between the crisp snap and the mellow whipped cream filling makes the cookies excellent palate cleansers or accompaniments for aperitifs. For added flair, top brandy snaps with shaved curls of chocolate or a sprig of mint.

Baking Notes: Use perfectly flat cookie sheets so that the cookies are as well formed as possible. You can also form brandy snaps by draping the warm cookies in teacups or muffin tins to create cup shapes.

Recipe: ¹/₂ cup all-purpose flour
¹/₂ teaspoon ground ginger
¹/₈ teaspoon salt
4 tablespoons unsalted butter
¹/₄ cup sugar
2 tablespoons light molasses
1 teaspoon brandy
¹/₂ teaspoon lemon juice

Filling:
2 cups heavy cream
3 tablespoons confectioners' sugar
4 teaspoons brandy
2 ounces semisweet chocolate, grated, for decoration

 1. Preheat oven to 325°F. Grease several cookie sheets or line with silicone baking mats.

 2. Sift flour, ginger, and salt into a medium bowl and set aside.

 3. In a small saucepan, melt butter, sugar and molasses together over medium heat, whisking constantly until the mixture is completely combined.

4. Remove from heat and let cool to room temperature.

5. Pour butter mixture into the flour mixture and whisk to combine.

6. Add brandy and lemon juice and whisk to combine.

7. Drop tablespoonfuls of dough onto cookie sheets. Do not put more than 4 cookies onto each sheet; space them as far apart as possible, as they will spread out. Using a wet hand, flatten the batter out slightly.

8. Bake for 7 to 9 minutes until they are golden brown.

9. Cool sheets on wire racks for a couple minutes before removing cookies with a metal spatula. Working quickly, roll brandy snaps around the handle of a wooden spoon to form a cone or tube shape. Place cookies back on wire racks to finish cooling.

10. For the filling: Use a stand mixer with the whisk attachment to whip cream on medium speed until soft peaks form.

11. Add confectioners' sugar slowly, and then the brandy. Whip until stiff peaks form.

12. Spoon whipped cream into brandy snaps directly or fill a pastry bag with the whipped cream and pipe

**into brandy snaps. Sprinkle with grated chocolate
and serve immediately.**

Yield: About 2 dozen cookies

Storage: Store unfilled cookies in an airtight container for up
          to 5 days.

CHICKASAW PUMPKIN COOKIES

General
Description: *These cookies, taken from the contemporary cooking tra-
              dition of the Chickasaw tribe, exemplify the unique
              blend of old and new in Native American cuisine.*
              While these cookies are similar in shape to many
              other drop cookies, they are distinguished by their
              rich copper tone and exciting, dynamic flavor.

History: The pumpkin has been an important element of the
              American Indian diet for millennia. Dale Carson, in
              New Native American Cooking, describes traditional
              Native cuisine as something of a misnomer due to
              the diversity of pre-Columbian cultures, the tragic
              loss of much of their traditions, and the change that
              nonnative foods effected in the culinary traditions of
              the Americas. For this reason, "Native cuisine" in
              the United States is typified by a combination of
              innovative and traditional ingredients.

Serving Suggestions:	These cookies are traditionally served in the fall, when pumpkins are harvested, although pumpkin puree can be obtained year-round.

Baking Notes:

Pumpkin puree can be bought canned or prepared at home by boiling the pumpkin in water with a dash of salt until fork tender, then blending in a stand mixer until an even consistency is reached. Ginger is best used fresh, but powdered ginger can be substituted—simply add it to the flour in step 4. Mix in chocolate chips for a touch of sweetness.

Recipe:

2¹/₂ cups minus 2 teaspoons all-purpose flour
4 teaspoons baking powder
³/₄ teaspoon salt
¹/₂ teaspoon ground nutmeg
¹/₂ teaspoon ground cinnamon
¹/₂ cup softened unsalted butter
1¹/₄ cups light brown sugar
2 eggs
1¹/₂ cups pumpkin puree
¹/₄ teaspoon finely grated fresh ginger
1 teaspoon vanilla extract
1 teaspoon lemon juice
1 cup raisins
1 cup chopped pecans

 1.   **Preheat oven to 400°F. Grease several cookie sheets.**

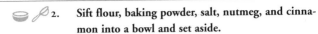

2. Sift flour, baking powder, salt, nutmeg, and cinnamon into a bowl and set aside.

3. In a stand mixer, cream butter and brown sugar on medium speed for several minutes until light and fluffy.

4. Add eggs, pumpkin, ginger, vanilla, and lemon juice; mix at medium speed to combine.

5. Gradually add flour mixture and mix at low speed until combined.

6. Fold in raisins and pecans by hand.

7. Drop tablespoon-sized balls of dough onto sheets about 1¹/₂ inches apart. Bake for 15 minutes or until the cookies are bronze in color, rotating cookie sheets halfway through. Cool sheets on wire racks for 5 minutes before transferring cookies directly onto wire racks with a metal spatula to finish cooling.

Yield: About 3 dozen cookies

Storage: Store in an airtight container for up to 1 week.

8a–b. **CHINESE ALMOND COOKIES**

General
Description:

This traditional Chinese-American cookie is light and crispy with a mild buttery, nutty flavor. It has a shiny, crackly top and is often decorated with sliced almonds. The cookie's shiny, golden appearance comes from the egg glaze applied to the top before baking, although yellow food coloring may be added to enhance the color. The cookies are traditionally made with lard but can be made with butter or shortening. They are often served at Chinese restaurants at the end of the meal, along with orange slices, or given as hostess gifts or party treats.

History:

Chinese immigrants to America adapted the traditional Chinese walnut cookie into the popular almond cookie in the 1800s. In America, April 9 has been designated National Chinese Almond Cookie Day. Twin Dragon, one of the most enduring commercial makers of Chinese almond cookies, packages them in pink boxes tied with red string. These iconic cookie boxes are sold in nearly every Chinese grocery store year-round.

Serving
Suggestions:

The cookie is a natural partner to Chinese teas, especially oolong or green teas. It is traditionally served with fresh apple or orange slices.

Baking Notes:

The cookie dough adapts well to Asian spices like

ginger, Chinese five spice, or star anise. The almonds
in Chinese almond cookies can be replaced with
other nuts, such as walnuts or pine nuts. Many
Chinese almond cookie recipes call for only regular
flour, although some ground almonds enhance the
sweet nuttiness of the cookie: try substituting $1/2$ cup
of the flour with $1/2$ cup of ground almond to
increase the almond flavor.

Recipe: **3 cups all-purpose flour**
1 cup sugar
1 teaspoon baking soda
$1/2$ teaspoon salt
1 cup softened unsalted butter
1 egg
$1^1/2$ teaspoons almond extract
$1/2$ cup sliced almonds for decoration
1 egg, beaten for egg wash

 1. **Sift flour, sugar, baking soda, and salt into a medium bowl and set aside.**

 2. **In a stand mixer with the paddle attachment, beat butter on medium speed until smooth.**

 3. **Add the egg and almond extract, and mix until combined.**

 4. **Add the flour mixture and mix on low speed until**

just combined.

 5. Turn out dough onto a piece of plastic wrap, and form into a disk. Cover dough and refrigerate for about 20 minutes until firm.

 6. Preheat the oven to 325°F. Grease several cookie sheets or line them with parchment paper.

 7. Roll the dough into 1-inch balls and place on the sheets about 1 inch apart. Flatten them with the palm of your hand.

 8. Place a sliced almond in the center of each ball of dough. Brush a little of the egg wash over the top of each cookie. Bake for 12 to 15 minutes, rotating cookie sheets halfway through; the cookies will start to turn golden at the edges when done. Cool sheets on wire racks for a few minutes before transferring cookies to wire racks to finish cooling.

Yield: About 3 dozen cookies

Storage: Keep cookies in an airtight container for up to 1 week.

Variation: ***Chinese Walnut Cookies***
Walnut trees are indigenous to China, and walnuts have been used in Chinese cuisine for centuries.

Substitute the sliced almond topping with $1/2$ cup toasted walnut halves. For a more intense walnut flavor, replace $1/2$ cup of the flour with $1/2$ cup ground toasted walnuts.

9a–b.

CHOCOLATE CHIP COOKIES

General Description:

With its familiar round shape, deep golden brown color, and chocolate chips studded throughout, the chocolate chip cookie is one of the most common American cookies. The popularity of these cookies is due to its ease of creation and near-universal appeal to the palate. Varying from thick and cakey to thin and chewy, chocolate chip cookies are characterized by a rich, vanilla flavor. The chocolate chip cookie is a favorite of children and adults alike, and can be found in homey or gourmet incarnations.

History:

The creation of the chocolate chip cookie is credited to Ruth Wakefield, the owner of the Toll House Inn in Whitman, Massachusetts. Wakefield was famous for her homemade cookies. One day she added broken pieces of chocolate to the batter, thinking they would melt and create chocolate dough. Instead, the pieces of chocolate stayed intact, and the chocolate chip cookie was created. In 1939, Nestle bought the rights to Wakefield's recipe, and a version of it appears on every bag of Nestle chocolate chips. This

commercial version, known as the Toll House
Chocolate Chip cookie, is one of the most well-
known and often used recipes in America.

Serving
Suggestions:

A glass of cold milk is a warm chocolate chip cookie's
classic companion. Although this cookie is best
served fresh from the oven, it is common to reheat a
cooled chocolate chip cookie in a microwave oven to
recapture the just-baked sensation. The cookie
adapts well to additional flavors, and many variations of chocolate chip cookies contain ingredients
such as oatmeal, peanut butter, pecans, walnuts, or
raisins. The chocolate in this cookie was traditionally
a semisweet chocolate chip; today, however, gourmet
versions contain rough chunks of premium, high
cacao–content chocolate.

Baking Notes:

Depending on ingredient proportions and baking
time, the chocolate chip cookie can vary from thick
to flat and from soft to chewy. Most people have a
definite preference for a particular style of chocolate
chip cookie, and it is easy to adapt the recipe to
achieve the desired result. For softer cookies, bake
them on the shorter side of the recommended time;
remove the cookies from the oven when they are just
starting to brown at the edges and the centers still
look slightly gooey. For crisper cookies, leave them
in the oven a few minutes longer than the recommended time. However, do not leave cookies in the

oven until they are completely dark, as they will overbake and harden once they have cooled. To create thinner, chewier cookies, reduce the amount of flour to ³/4 cup.

Recipe:
1¹/3 cups all-purpose flour
¹/2 teaspoon baking soda
¹/2 teaspoon salt
¹/2 cup softened unsalted butter
¹/3 cup sugar
¹/2 cup light brown sugar
1 egg
³/4 teaspoon vanilla extract
1 cup (6 oz) chocolate chips

 1. Preheat the oven to 350°F. Line several cookie sheets with parchment paper or silicone baking mats.

 2. Sift the flour, baking soda, and salt into a bowl and set aside.

 3. In a stand mixer, cream butter and sugars on medium speed for several minutes until light and fluffy. Add the egg and vanilla and mix until combined.

 4. Add the flour mixture, and mix on low speed just until combined; add the chocolate chips, and mix until evenly distributed.

5.   **Drop tablespoon-sized balls of dough onto cookie sheets about 2 inches apart.**

6.   **Bake for 8 to 10 minutes, rotating sheets halfway through. Cool sheets on wire racks for a few minutes before transferring cookies directly onto wire racks with a spatula to finish cooling.**

Yield: About 2 dozen cookies

Storage: Store in an airtight container for up to a week.

Variations: ***Chocolate Chip Toffee Cookies***
Add approximately 1/2 cup (4 oz) chopped Heath bars or toffee bits when you mix the chocolate chips into the dough in step 4.

Chocolate Chip Ice Cream Sandwiches
Chocolate chip cookies are perfect for making your own ice cream sandwiches. Flavors that go well with chocolate chip include vanilla, coffee, or butter pecan. Let the ice cream sit out at room temperature for a few minutes to soften. Turn half of the cookies upside down, and spread a thick layer of ice cream on each of them. Press the other cookies on top and press down lightly to form sandwiches. Serve immediately or cover in plastic wrap and freeze for up to 3 days. Decorate ice cream sandwiches by pressing sprinkles, chocolate chips, or nuts into the ice cream.

10.   **CHOCOLATE CRINKLES**

General
Description:
The chocolate crinkle is a soft, fudgy cookie covered in confectioners' sugar that has "cracked" on top to show the dark brown chocolate interior. Its appearance results from a ball of the dark chocolate crinkle dough being rolled in confectioners' sugar before baking; as the cookie expands in the oven, cracks and crinkles form in the sugar, revealing the chocolate beneath. The cookie has a very thin crackly top crust underneath the confectioners' sugar, but the interior is rich and moist, almost like a brownie, and it has a deep chocolate flavor from the chocolate and cocoa powder in the dough. Chocolate crinkles are also known as *black and whites* (not to be confused with **black and white cookies**) or *cookies in the snow.*

History:
Chocolate crinkles started appearing in American cookbooks in the 1950s. Their sweetness, soft, chewy texture, and catchy name are characteristic of the typical American cookie. Other cookie recipes that call for similar techniques include **snickerdoodles** and **molasses spice cookies**, which are rolled in granulated sugar before baking.

Serving
Suggestions:
The chocolate crinkle is a popular cookie during the winter holidays because of its snowy appearance. The cookie can be made even more festive by substituting peppermint extract for the vanilla in the recipe. The

dough balls can also be rolled in granulated sugar instead of confectioners' sugar for a different appearance. Chocolate crinkles go well with a tall glass of milk or a mug of coffee.

Baking Notes:

This cookie is a showcase for chocolate, so use the best quality chocolate and cocoa powder available. Semisweet or bittersweet chocolate works best. Do not use milk chocolate or chocolate chips. The dough softens very quickly once removed from the refrigerator; do not be afraid to put the dough back in to chill if it becomes too soft. Chocolate crinkles are meant to be soft and almost gooey in the center, so don't overbake them. If you are not getting a "cracked" top after baking, you may not be covering the dough balls with enough confectioners' sugar. It's best to bake these cookies one cookie sheet at a time, as baking several sheets together may affect the airflow in the oven and prevent them from developing their signature crackled tops.

Recipe:

6 oz semisweet chocolate, chopped into small pieces

$1/4$ cup plus 2 tablespoons softened unsalted butter

$1/2$ cup sugar

2 eggs

1 teaspoon vanilla extract

$1^1/2$ cups all-purpose flour

2 tablespoons cocoa powder

³/₄ teaspoon baking powder
¹/₄ teaspoon salt
Confectioners' sugar for rolling

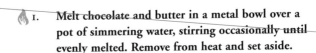

1. Melt chocolate and butter in a metal bowl over a pot of simmering water, stirring occasionally until evenly melted. Remove from heat and set aside.

2. In a stand mixer, beat sugar and eggs on medium speed for several minutes until thick and smooth. Add the vanilla extract and melted chocolate mixture, and beat on medium-low until combined.

3. Sift flour, cocoa, baking powder, and salt into a bowl.

4. Add flour mixture, and mix until combined.

5. Cover dough and chill in refrigerator for about 2 hours or until firm enough to scoop.

6. Preheat the oven to 325°F. Line several cookie sheets with parchment paper or silicone baking mats.

7. Roll 1-inch balls of dough in confectioners' sugar, coating completely; place balls about 1¹/₂ inches apart on cookie sheets. Bake for 8 to 10 minutes, rotating sheets halfway through, until they just start to feel firm. Cool sheets on wire racks for about 5

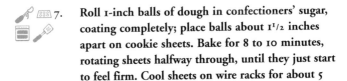

**minutes before transferring cookies directly onto
wire racks with a metal spatula to finish cooling.**

Yield: About 4 dozen cookies

Storage: Store flat in an airtight container for up to 2 days.
These cookies should be served quickly, as the confectioners' sugar will melt over time.

11.   **CHOCOLATE ESPRESSO COOKIES**

General
Description: *These soft, dark, buzz-worthy cookies pack a double
punch of chocolate and espresso.* They are similar to
triple chocolate cookies, but the strong bite of espresso and the rich mocha flavor set these cookies apart.

History: Although the two main ingredients of these cookies
originated on opposite ends of the globe, both have
long been important to culinary tradition. Cacao
trees, from which chocolate is produced, were first
cultivated in the Amazon more than 3,000 years ago.
The word *chocolate* comes from the Nahuatl term
xocolatl, which means "bitter water," as chocolate was
originally consumed ceremonially as a kind of tea.
Coffee beans, on the other hand, have been cultivated only for the last 1,000 years. The origins of coffee
are in Ethiopia, where goatherds apparently noticed
the effects of these beans in the jumpy, excitable

goats who ate them.

Serving
Suggestions:

These rich, soft cookies are a perfect way to jump-start a day. Both of the main ingredients are great sources of quick energy: cocoa contains small amounts of stimulating alkaloids and caffeine, and espresso's caffeine jolt is legendary.

Baking Notes:

For variety, substitute part (or all) of the semisweet chocolate chips with white chocolate chips. Or substitute the chocolate chips with chopped hazelnuts and chopped dried cherries. Decaffeinated espresso can be substituted for regular espresso.

Recipe:

1 3/4 cups all-purpose flour
3 tablespoons cocoa powder
2 1/2 teaspoons instant espresso powder
1 3/4 teaspoons baking powder
1/4 teaspoon salt
12 oz semisweet chocolate
1/2 cup softened unsalted butter
1 cup dark brown sugar
1/2 cup sugar
3 eggs
1 teaspoon vanilla extract
1 cup (6 oz) chocolate chips

 1. **Sift flour, cocoa powder, espresso powder, baking powder, and salt into a bowl and set aside.**

2. Melt chocolate in a metal bowl set over a pot of simmering water, stirring occasionally so it will melt evenly; remove from heat when smooth.

 3. In a stand mixer, cream butter and sugars on medium speed for several minutes until light and fluffy. Add eggs and vanilla and mix until combined.

 4. Pour in melted chocolate and beat until combined.

 5. Add flour mixture and chocolate chips and mix on low just until incorporated.

 6. Cover dough and refrigerate for about 15–20 minutes until it is firm enough to scoop.

 7. Preheat the oven to 350°F. Line several cookie sheets with parchment paper or silicone baking mats.

 8. Roll dough into 1¹/₂-inch balls and place on sheets about 2 inches apart.

 9. Bake for 8 to 10 minutes—cookies will still appear soft but will firm up upon cooling. Cool cookie sheets on wire racks before removing cookies with a metal spatula.

Yield: About 5 dozen cookies

Storage: Store in an airtight container for up to 2 weeks.

12. **COCONUT MACAROONS**

General
Description: *The coconut macaroon is a soft, chewy cookie made of shredded coconut bound together with egg whites and sugar.* It should not be confused with the **French macaron** or other macaroon cookies from Europe. The coconut macaroon is so widely known in North America that it is often referred to as a *macaroon* without the coconut descriptor. Coconut macaroons usually look like small mounds or are sometimes formed in a "haystack" shape; the outside layer of coconut turns crisp and brown from the sugar caramelizing in the oven, while the inside is soft, moist, and chewy. They are associated with Passover, as they require no leaveners and can be made with kosher ingredients.

History: Coconut macaroons were probably adapted from Italian macaroons made with almonds, known as **amaretti**. Since the flourless coconut macaroon can be eaten at Passover, the recipe spread through Jewish communities across Eastern Europe. These cookies traveled to America with immigrant families, where coconut replaced almonds and they became a part of America's culinary traditions.

Serving
Suggestions:

Coconut macaroons are a traditional Passover sweet, but they are a welcome treat anytime. For a dramatic presentation, dip the tops of macaroons in melted chocolate.

Baking Notes:

For perfectly round mounds, use an ice cream or cookie scoop to drop the balls of dough onto cookie sheets. If you need to fix loose pieces of coconut or smooth out edges, wet your hands before working with the mounds of batter.

Recipe:

2 egg whites
¹/₂ cup sugar
1 teaspoon vanilla extract
1¹/₂ cups sweetened flaked coconut

1. **Combine all ingredients in a medium metal or glass bowl with a rubber spatula.**

2. **Place the bowl over a pot of gently simmering water; cook the mixture, stirring often, for about 20–25 minutes. The goal is to dry out the wet mixture so that it holds its shape when scooped. When the mixture is ready, the sugar should have melted and the coconut should have absorbed all the liquid but still appear moist.**

3. **While the mixture is cooking, preheat the oven to 350°F and line several cookie sheets with parchment**

paper or use silicone baking mats. These cookies will otherwise stick to a greased or floured pan.

 4. Use a cookie scoop or small ice cream scoop to portion out the dough. Fill the scoop completely and level off the top before dispensing onto the cookie sheet to get a perfect dome. Space cookies about 1 inch apart. Bake for 14 to 16 minutes, rotating sheets halfway through. The macaroons will turn golden brown on the outside; do not let them overbake or the macaroons will lose their signature moist, chewy texture. Completely cool cookie sheets on wire racks; then gently peel off the macaroons, taking care not to break them.

Yield: About 2 dozen macaroons

Storage: Store in an airtight container for up to 1 week.

COWBOY COOKIES

13a–b.

General Description: *Like all things Texas, these cookies are bigger and better than most.* Cowboy cookies are typically oversized and stuffed chock-full of mix-ins, from raisins to chocolate chips.

History: Cowboy cookies are most popular in Texas, but they

are also a favorite in California. First Lady Laura Bush's family recipe for cowboy cookies competed with Tipper Gore's **gingersnap** recipe during the 2000 presidential election. Cowboy cookies may be related to ranger cookies, which are bigger and better **chocolate chip cookies** stuffed with a hodge-podge of mix-ins: rolled oats, shredded coconut, nuts, and even cornflakes.

Serving Suggestions:

For a taste of the Wild West, serve cowboy cookies with a steaming cup of spicy Mexican hot chocolate.

Baking Notes:

Walnuts can be substituted with pecans or other nuts, and other mix-ins like shredded coconut, white chocolate chips, or raisins. Add spices for a spicy-sweet cowboy cookie (page 52).

Recipe:

2 cups all purpose flour
1 teaspoon baking soda
1/2 teaspoon baking powder
1/2 teaspoon salt
1 cup softened unsalted butter
1/2 cup sugar
1/2 cup light brown sugar
2 eggs
1 teaspoon vanilla extract
13/4 cups rolled oats
11/2 cups (9 ounces) semisweet chocolate chips

1 cup chopped walnuts

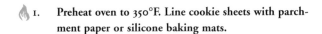

1. Preheat oven to 350°F. Line cookie sheets with parchment paper or silicone baking mats.

2. Sift flour, baking soda, baking powder, and salt together into a bowl and set aside.

3. In a stand mixer, cream butter and sugars on medium speed for several minutes until light and fluffy. Add the eggs and vanilla and mix until combined.

4. Add the flour mixture and mix on low speed until just combined.

5. Stir in oats, chocolate chips, and walnuts with a wooden spoon.

6. Scoop out dough with a 1/4 cup measure or a big ice cream scoop. Place on cookie sheets about 2 inches apart. Flatten with the palm of your hand.

7. Bake for 14 to 16 minutes, rotating halfway through. The cookies are done when they are golden brown and the tops look firm. Cool sheets on wire racks.

Yield: About 2 dozen cookies

Storage: Store in an airtight container for up to a week.

Variation: ***Spicy Cowboy Cookies***

For a spicy variation on this classic, add 1 teaspoon
cinnamon, 1/2 teaspoon ginger, and 1/2–3/4 teaspoon
cayenne pepper to the flour mixture (3/4 teaspoon
will make a fairly spicy cookie). Proceed with rest of
the recipe as directed.

14.   **FLORENTINES**

General   *Florentines are thin, crisp, candy-like cookies topped with*
Description: *nuts, candied citrus, and glace cherries, with a thin layer*
of tempered chocolate on the bottom. Although they
may resemble **tuiles**, florentines are made differently;
they do not contain eggs, and are made by cooking
honey, sugar, and cream together. Baked, cooled
Florentines can be spread on one side with a layer of
tempered chocolate, and a wavy design marked in
the chocolate with a fork. Florentines can also be
made like a bar cookie, with the hot sugar mixture
poured over a prebaked nutty crust and melted
chocolate drizzled over the top. These ingredients
and preparation methods give florentines a caramel-
ly, candylike flavor and pleasingly chewy texture.
Their elaborate appearance makes florentines a popular cookie for the holidays.

History: Florentines have long been associated with Italy but
Austria also claims to have invented them. The

process of candying fruit was developed in the 14th century as a way to preserve fruit or the peel of fruit. When soaked in a sugar syrup, pieces of fruit become saturated with sugar, which prevents the growth of mold. Since candying fruit extended its life beyond summer, it is not surprising that it became popular in holiday desserts.

Serving
Suggestions:

Traditional florentines are coated with chocolate underneath, but if you're not inclined to temper chocolate, simply drizzle the tops of the cookies with melted chocolate.

Baking Notes:

Be sure to use parchment paper or silicone baking mats on the cookie sheets to prevent the cookies from sticking. If the batter is too runny to shape cookies before baking, simply return the mixture to the stove and cook a few minutes more until the desired consistency is reached. If batter becomes too thick and does not spread easily, add more cream, about 1–2 teaspoons at a time.

Recipe:

1 cup softened unsalted butter
1¹/₄ cups sugar
2 tablespoons corn syrup
1 tablespoon all-purpose flour
¹/₃ cup heavy cream
¹/₄ teaspoon salt
2¹/₃ cups sliced almonds

4 oz roughly chopped bittersweet chocolate
(optional)

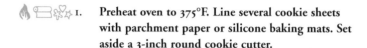

1.   Preheat oven to 375°F. Line several cookie sheets
     with parchment paper or silicone baking mats. Set
     aside a 3-inch round cookie cutter.

2.   In a medium saucepan, melt butter, sugar, and
     corn syrup together over medium heat.

3.   Add flour and stir to combine; add cream and salt
     and stir to combine.

4.   Continue to cook until mixture comes to a boil.
     Add the almonds and stir to combine.

5.   Continue cooking, stirring constantly, for about 3
     minutes, until mixture thickens and moves around
     pan as one mass. Remove from heat.

6.   Drop spoonfuls of dough onto cookie sheets. Do
     not put more than 4 cookies on a cookie sheet;
     space them as far apart as possible, as the baked
     cookies will spread to about triple the area. Using
     an offset spatula or wet hand, spread and flatten
     batter into 3-inch rounds, creating a very thin
     layer. Continue wetting spatula or fingers with
     water if batter is sticky.

7. Bake for 5 to 8 minutes or until edges are brown and centers are slightly golden; don't worry if cookies begin to spread, as they will be reshaped later.

 8. Remove cookie sheets from oven and immediately reshape cookies back into 3-inch circles; use the cookie cutter to "scoop" batter back into place and round out edges. Cookies will begin to harden within a couple minutes—if they become too hard to reshape, return them to the oven for a minute or so.

 9. Cool reshaped cookies on sheets until they are firm and cool enough to handle. Then move them to a wire rack covered in parchment paper to cool completely.

 10. To finish (optional): Melt chocolate, either in the microwave or in a metal bowl over a pot of simmering water on the stove. Drizzle melted chocolate over the tops of the florentines. Allow chocolate to cool and harden before serving.

Yield: About 3 dozen cookies

Storage: Store florentines in an airtight container, layered between sheets of parchment or waxed paper. They should be eaten within 24 hours, after which they will begin to soften and lose their shape and texture.

15. **FRENCH MACARONS**

General
Description:

*One of the most enduring stars of the cookie pantheon, French macarons are a **meringue**-like cookie made of almond flour, confectioners' sugar, and whipped egg whites.* They are small, round, and characterized by a smooth domed top and a ruffled base often known as a "foot." Macarons have a light, thin crust that gives way to a soft, barely chewy center. In Paris, macarons are assembled in pairs with a filling of ganache or buttercream. Other regions of France have local versions of macarons, which are usually closer to the cookie's simple origins: a single cookie, light golden in color and tasting of almonds. *Luxemburgerli* or *Luxembourger* are Swiss cookies that resemble a small French macaron; they are based on the original French recipe.

History:

Macarons did not become popular in France until the French Revolution, when two nuns escaping the dissolution of their church took refuge in the city of Nancy and baked macarons to support themselves. They became known as the "Macaron sisters," and the cookie's popularity spread throughout the region. In the early 1900s, Pierre Desfontaines, cousin of the famous French pâtissiere Louis Ladurée, came up with the idea of sandwiching two macarons together with ganache, and the *macaron parisien* was born.

Serving
Suggestions:

With their tiny size and elegant shape, macarons are the perfect petit-four. They can be made in a variety of flavors and colors for an impressive presentation. The easiest way to do this is to tint the macaron dough and flavor the buttercream filling. A box of macarons always makes an elegant gift.

Baking Notes:

In order to achieve perfectly smooth, domed tops, it is important to grind the almonds to a very fine powder. Purchase almond meal premade, or grind whole blanched almonds in the food processor. Use almonds that have had their skins removed, or the dark flecks will tint the macarons. Sift the confectioners' sugar so there are no lumps. When folding the ground almond and confectioners' sugar mixture into the whipped egg whites, incorporate it as gently as possible to avoid deflating the batter; retain as much air as possible. If it looks like the batter is too stiff, let it sit for 5–10 minutes to let the batter relax and soften slightly before piping. Be aware that the batter will soften as you pipe it, so you don't want it too runny at the beginning. If it is too runny, the only recourse is to pipe the macarons as small as possible so they do not spread into giant circles. When piping macarons, release the piping pressure first, then end the piping motion by tucking the end to the side instead of pulling straight up (that leaves a point sticking up that is difficult to flatten). Since macarons are made with a meringue, beware of bad weather; if it is a humid, wet day, macarons are likely to deflate and become sticky. They are most successfully made on dry days.

Recipe: **1 cup almond meal or ground blanched almonds**
1¹/₄ cups confectioners' sugar
3 egg whites
¹/₄ cup sugar

Filling:
¹/₄ cup softened unsalted butter
¹/₄ cup confectioners' sugar
2 tablespoons almond meal or ground blanched almonds

 1. Using a food processor, grind almond meal and confectioners' sugar until the almond meal is as fine as possible.

 2. Sift almond-sugar mixture, and throw out any pieces that do not fit through the strainer; set aside sifted mixture.

 3. Line several cookie sheets with parchment paper. Do not use insulated cookie sheets.

 4. Using a stand mixer with the whisk attachment, whisk egg whites on medium-low speed until foamy.

5. Increase the mixer's speed to medium (no higher), and add sugar in a slow stream, pausing a few times to let the sugar incorporate. Continue to whisk egg whites and sugar until they form soft to medium peaks. Whisk by hand at the final stages; if you whip too far to stiff peaks, simply set the whites aside for a few minutes and allow them to relax.

 6. Transfer egg whites to a large bowl. Sprinkle $1/3$ the almond-sugar mixture evenly over the egg whites. Using a large rubber spatula or bowl scraper, gently fold it in. Combine thoroughly, then add another $1/3$, fold, add $1/3$, and fold.

 7. Fit a pastry bag with a large plain tip. Fill pastry bag about half full with macaron batter. Dab a little macaron batter underneath the corners of the parchment paper on the cookie sheets to act as a glue to keep the paper in place.

 8. Pipe discs about $1^{1}/_{2}$ inches in diameter, $1^{1}/_{2}$ inches apart, on the parchment-lined sheets. Finish piping of each cookie with a quick turn of the wrist. It may be helpful to place a weight on the parchment so it does not move when lifting up the piping bag.

 9. After piping all of the macarons, set them aside for 30 minutes until the tops set and form a shell. Meanwhile, preheat the oven to 375°F.

10. Place a second cookie sheet under the prepared sheets, doubling up the pans, and bake for 5 minutes (the second sheet will help the macarons rise properly and create the signature "foot").

11. Remove the second sheet, rotate the cookie sheets, and turn the oven down to 300°F; bake for 5 more minutes. Remove cookie sheets from oven and cool on wire racks; once cool, slowly remove cookies by pulling the parchment gently from macarons.

12. For the filling: In a small mixing bowl, beat butter until smooth. Add confectioners' sugar and almond meal, and mix until combined.

13. To assemble macarons: Pair up macarons, matching by similar size. Spread a thin layer of the filling on one flat side of each pair, about ⅛ inch thick. Create a sandwich with the other macaron.

Yield:　16 sandwiches (or 32 individual cookies)

Storage:　Macarons are best served the same day, but can be frozen unfilled for up to two weeks. To freeze, wrap tightly in plastic wrap and be careful—they are very fragile! Let them come to room temperature before filling.

16. 📷   **HERMIT COOKIES**

General
Description:
Similar to Southern tea cakes but with distinctive brown coloring and strong spiced flavor, hermits are a classic New England dessert. Their form has varied widely, but hermits always contain a variety of spices, dried fruit, and nuts. They have a rich, spicy taste similar to other spice cookies, but the raisins and other mix-ins studded throughout the dough gives them a chunky, craggy appearance. Their texture also ranges from dense and moist to dry and firm. Hermits are often made drop-style, but they are also made in a pan and cut into bars, or shaped into logs and sliced into thick pieces. The flavor of hermits actually improves a few days after baking, which may be one of the reasons for their name—these solitary cookies need some "alone time" before coming out to dinner.

History:
It has been suggested that the cookies take their name from the brown sack-clothes purportedly worn by old hermits. Alternately, the cookies may have arrived in American baking by way of Moravian immigrants to Pennsylvania and North Carolina; their famous rolled, flat spiced cookies called **Moravian spice cookies** are known in their native German as *Herrnhuter*, which may have eventually Anglicized into the familiar *hermit*. Exactly how long hermits have been around is hard to say, but they made their first printed appearance in a cookbook

from Maine in 1877. They are especially popular in Northeastern Canada and the Eastern United States.

Serving Suggestions:

Hermit dough adapts to whichever extras strike your fancy. Instead of raisins, try cranberries, pecans, chocolate chips, or currants. Simply keep the proportions of mix-in ingredients the same.

Baking Notes:

Make hermits a few days ahead of time, or take them as snacks for a long trip.

Recipe

1³/₄ cups all-purpose flour
¹/₂ teaspoon baking soda
¹/₂ teaspoon salt
¹/₂ teaspoon ground nutmeg
¹/₂ teaspoon ground cinnamon
¹/₂ cup softened unsalted butter
1 cup light brown sugar
1 egg
¹/₄ cup buttermilk at room temperature
1 cup raisins
1 cup chopped walnuts

 1. Sift flour, baking soda, salt, nutmeg, and cinnamon into a bowl and set aside.

 2. In a stand mixer, cream butter and brown sugar together on medium speed for several minutes until smooth.

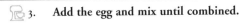 3. Add the egg and mix until combined.

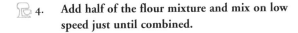 4. Add half of the flour mixture and mix on low
speed just until combined.

5. Add the buttermilk slowly, and continue mixing
until combined. Add the remaining half of the
flour mixture and mix on low speed until well
combined. Fold in raisins and walnuts by hand.

6. Cover dough and chill in refrigerator for 1 hour.

7. Preheat the oven to 350°F. Grease several cookie
sheets or line them with parchment paper.

8. Drop teaspoonfuls of dough onto sheets about 2
inches apart on the sheets. Bake in the oven for 10
to 12 minutes, rotating sheets halfway through.
Cookies should be lightly golden and no imprint
will remain when touched in the center. Cool
sheets on wire racks for a few minutes before
transferring cookies directly onto wire racks with a
metal spatula to finish cooling.

Yield: About 3 dozen cookies

Storage: Store in an airtight container for up to 1 week or
freeze in an airtight container for up to 3 weeks.
Defrost cookies in container on counter overnight.

17. **JUMBLES**

General
Description:

Chock-full of nuts and scented with oranges, these jumbles are a modern take on a very old English cookie. The original jumbles were predecessors to today's **sugar cookies**, but variations of classic jumbles are still made and enjoyed today. The unusual addition of sour cream gives these hodge-podge cookies a particularly soft texture, with a crunch of nuts throughout.

History:

Jumbles, alternately spelled *jumbals* or *jumballs*, are hallmark cookies in early American baking. These cookies may predate the modern usage of the word *jumble*, with references dating back to 1615 England. They were popular in the kitchen of America's first First Lady, Martha Washington.

Serving
Suggestions:

Since the ingredient list is so flexible, jumbles are a good last-minute option for dessert; they are excellent everyday cookies but also Christmas cookies.

Baking Notes:

Jumbles are the ultimate mix-in cookie. Toss in chocolate chips, sweetened coconut flakes, crispy rice cereal, raisins, or other nuts—just make sure your total amount of mix-ins doesn't exceed 2 cups.

Recipe:

2 3/4 cups all-purpose flour
1/2 teaspoon baking soda
1 teaspoon salt

$^1/_2$ cup softened unsalted butter
$1^1/_2$ cups light brown sugar
2 eggs
$1^1/_2$ teaspoons vanilla extract
2 teaspoons orange zest
1 cup sour cream
1 cup chopped pecans

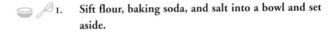

1. Sift flour, baking soda, and salt into a bowl and set aside.

2. In a stand mixer, cream butter and sugar until light and fluffy. Add the eggs, vanilla, and orange zest and mix until combined.

3. Add half of the flour mixture, and mix on low speed until just combined; add sour cream, and mix until combined. Add the rest of the flour mixture, and mix until combined.

4. Fold in pecans by hand.

5. Cover dough and refrigerate for 30 minutes until firm.

6. Preheat the oven to 350°F. Line several cookie sheets with parchment paper or silicone baking mats.

7. Drop tablespoon-sized balls of dough onto cookie sheets about 2 inches apart.

8. **Bake for 8 to 10 minutes, rotating sheets halfway through. Cool sheets on wire racks for a few minutes before transferring cookies directly onto wire racks with a spatula to finish cooling.**

Yield: About 4 dozen cookies

Storage: Store in a single layer in an airtight container for up to 1 week.

---

 18. **LACE COOKIES**

General Description: *These crispy classics take their name from the delicate perforations spread across their thin, almost transparent surface.* As beautiful as they are tasty, lace cookies appear to require more work than they actually do. Their texture varies from thin and crispy to delicately lacy and crispy.

History: Lace cookies have been popular for centuries in Ireland, Scotland, Switzerland, France, and in the Netherlands, where they are known as *klets koekjes*. Today, many variations have become popular worldwide, from pecan lace to oatmeal lace cookies.

Serving Suggestions: Serve lace cookies with strawberries and fresh whipped cream for an elegant summer dessert. Lace cookies can be dipped in melted chocolate and then cooled, given a citrus flavor with a teaspoon of orange zest added to the dough, or curled into tuile shapes when they are fresh out of the oven.

Baking Notes: Use perfectly flat cookie sheets so that the cookies are as well formed as possible. They are quite fragile, so handle and store them with care. If they become soft, they can be re-crisped in the oven.

Recipe:
4 tablespoons unsalted butter
6 tablespoons dark brown sugar
$1/4$ cup light corn syrup
3 tablespoons all-purpose flour
$1^1/2$ teaspoons heavy cream
$1/2$ teaspoon vanilla extract
$1/8$ teaspoon salt
$1/2$ cup finely chopped pecans

1. **In a small saucepan, melt butter, sugar and corn syrup together over medium heat, whisking constantly until the mixture begins to boil.**

2. **Remove from heat. Add flour and stir to combine.**

3. **Add cream, vanilla, and salt and stir to combine.**

4. **Add nuts and stir until fully combined. Let mixture cool for 15 to 20 minutes.**

5. **Preheat oven to 350°F. Line several cookie sheets with parchment paper or silicone baking mats.**

 6. **Drop teaspoonfuls of dough onto cookie sheets. Do not put more than 3 cookies on a cookie sheet; space them as far apart as possible, as the baking cookies will spread out.**

 7. **Bake for 7 to 9 minutes until they are golden brown and stop bubbling.**

 8. **Cool sheets on wire racks for a few minutes before removing cookies with a metal spatula. Cookies will be very fragile so work carefully. Move cookies to parchment paper or wax paper to finish cooling.**

Yield: About 2 dozen cookies

Storage: Store in an airtight container, layered between sheets
    of parchment or waxed paper, for up to 5 days.

19a–b. ⬛   ## LAVENDER ORANGE PUFFS

General
Description: *Lightly dusted in powdered sugar, these puff cookies will scent a room with the elegant combination of lavender and citrus.* Lavender orange puff cookies are a unique, modern twist on the classic puff cookie.

History:	American puff cookies originated in the late 1800s. By this time, Americans were gaining access to a variety of baking ingredients and myriad puff cookies began to emerge, from raisin puff cookies to the popular **Amish puff cookies**.

Serving Suggestions:	These puffs are wonderfully suited to a cup of tea on a cool spring day or as dessert for a summer luncheon.

Baking Notes:	As they bake, these cookies puff before settling, giving them a crinkly appearance. Be sure the lavender you use is culinary grade and safe for consumption. As an alternative to powdering these cookies with confectioners' sugar, drizzle them with a lavender glaze (pages 70–1) once cool.

Recipe:

$1^1/2$ cups all-purpose flour

$1/2$ teaspoon baking powder

$1/2$ teaspoon baking soda

$1/2$ teaspoon cream of tartar

$1/4$ teaspoon salt

2 teaspoons finely chopped dried lavender

$1/2$ cup softened unsalted butter

$1/2$ cup light brown sugar

$1/4$ cup sugar

1 egg

$1^1/2$ teaspoons orange zest

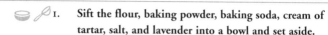 1. Sift the flour, baking powder, baking soda, cream of tartar, salt, and lavender into a bowl and set aside.

2. In a stand mixer, cream butter and sugars on medium speed for several minutes until light and fluffy. Add the egg and orange zest and mix until combined.

3. Add the flour mixture, and mix on low speed just until combined.

4. Cover dough and refrigerate for 30 minutes.

5. Preheat the oven to 375°F. Line several cookie sheets with parchment paper.

6. Drop tablespoon-sized balls of dough onto cookie sheets about 3 inches apart.

7. Bake for 8 to 10 minutes, rotating sheets halfway through, until golden brown. Cool cookie sheets on wire racks.

Yield:　About 2 dozen cookies

Storage:　Store in an airtight container for up to 1 week.

Variation:　***Lavender Glazed Puffs***
　　　　　　Drizzle this lavender glaze over the puffs for a glossy,

aromatic coating. If you cannot find lavender honey, any light honey will do.

2 tablespoons lavender honey
¹/₂ cup confectioners' sugar, sifted
1 tablespoon orange juice, room temperature

In a small saucepan, heat honey until warm and runny. Remove from heat and add confectioners' sugar and orange juice. Whisk thoroughly to combine. Lightly drizzle over cooled cookies. Let glaze set before serving.

20.   **MAHÓN CHEESE PUFFS (GOUGÈRES)**

General
Description:
The light, fluffy body of these scrumptious cheese puffs is balanced by the sharp, lingering bite of Mahón cheese. Mahón, a cheese made on the island of Minorca, has a singular flavor. The strong acidic taste of the cheese results from the high salt content in the island's soil, which is absorbed by the grasses upon which the island's cattle feed.

History:
Cheese puffs, or *gougères*, are a savory application of pâte à choux. See **profiteroles** for the history of this dough. *Gougères* are a specialty of Burgundy, France, and are classically made with Gruyère, a firm Swiss cheese.

Serving Suggestions:	Cheese puffs are elegant hors d'oeuvres at any dinner party. Fold in bits of ham or bacon into the batter for an even more savory delight.

Baking Notes:	To bring out the deliciously contrasting flavors of these puffs, it is best to use aged Mahón cheese. You can also substitute any hard cheese, such as Gruyère, Comté, or cheddar.

Recipe:

1 cup all-purpose flour
$^1/_2$ teaspoon salt
$^1/_2$ cup milk
5 tablespoons unsalted butter, cut into pieces
4 eggs (plus 1 if needed)
$^1/_2$ cup Mahón cheese, grated
1 egg, beaten, for egg wash

1. Preheat oven to 400°F. Line several cookie sheets with parchment paper or silicone baking mats.

2. Sift flour and salt into a medium bowl and set aside.

3. Combine milk, butter, salt, and $^1/_2$ cup of water in a medium saucepan and bring to a boil on medium heat.

4. Add the flour mixture all at once. Reduce heat to low and stir constantly with a wooden spoon until mixture forms a ball and pulls away from the sides of the pan, about 4–5 minutes.

5. Pour dough into a stand mixer and mix at medium speed for a few minutes to let the dough cool down.

6. Add the eggs one at a time, letting each one incorporate fully before adding the next one. The dough should become smooth, shiny, and slightly sticky. If the batter looks stiff and dry, add a fifth egg.

7. Fold in about 3/4 of the grated cheese into the dough. Be sure the dough has cooled down enough that it does not melt the cheese.

8. Fit a pastry bag with a large plain tip. Fill pastry bag about half full with pâte à choux dough. Dab a little dough underneath the corners of the parchment paper on the cookie sheets to act as a glue to keep the paper in place.

9. Pipe rounds of dough onto the cookie sheets about 2 inches apart. Brush each round with a little egg wash. Sprinkle the rest of the cheese over the rounds.

10. Bake for 10 minutes, until the rounds have started to puff and rise. Reduce heat to 350°F, rotate the sheets, and bake for about 10 to 15 minutes more, until the puffs have turned golden brown.

11. Remove puffs from oven and let cool slightly before serving.

Yield: About 3 dozen puffs

Storage: These puffs are best eaten right after they are made.
To store them, freeze cooled puffs for up to 1 week.
Defrost them and refresh in a 350°F oven before
serving.

 MAPLE COOKIES

21a–b.

General
Description: *With a soft, sugar-sprinkled body and the mellow flavor*
of real maple syrup, these golden cookies are favorites in
Canada and the American Northeast.

History: When British and French colonists first began to settle the eastern coast of North America, American
Indians introduced them to a sweet syrup derived
from the sap of the maple trees native to the region.
This sweetener allowed colonists to adapt the baking
traditions from home and provided a less expensive
alternative to sugar imported from the slave planta-
tions of the Caribbean.

Serving
Suggestions: Maple cookies are perfectly suited to a steaming cup
of hot chocolate or cider, whether spiked or nonalcoholic. If you can find maple sugar, sprinkle it on
the cookies instead of turbinado sugar for an extra
dose of maple flavor.

Baking Notes: Be sure to use real maple syrup, not imitation
"maple-flavored" syrup. Maple syrup comes in several
grades. In the United States, maple syrup usually
comes in two grades, A and B. In Canada, maple
syrup comes in grades #1 to #3. The grades corre-
spond to when in the season the syrup was made and
therefore the depth and intensity of its flavor. Grades
A and #1 are the first syrups of the season and therefore the lightest and mildest; Grades B, #2, and #3
are later syrups and have a darker, stronger flavor.
Usually Grades B and #2 are best suited for baking. If
you find the flavor too intense, use a lighter grade.

Recipe: 1¹/₂ cups all-purpose flour
¹/₂ teaspoon baking soda
¹/₂ teaspoon salt
¹/₂ cup softened unsalted butter
¹/₂ cup sugar
¹/₂ cup light brown sugar
1 egg
1 teaspoon vanilla extract
¹/₄ cup maple syrup
1 cup chopped pecans
Turbinado sugar or maple sugar for sprinkling

 1. Sift the flour, baking soda, and salt into a bowl and
set aside.

 2. In a stand mixer, cream butter and sugars on medium

speed for several minutes until light and fluffy. Add egg and vanilla, and mix until combined.

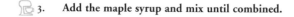 3. Add the maple syrup and mix until combined.

4. Add the flour mixture and mix on low until just combined. Fold in the pecans by hand.

5. Cover dough and chill in the refrigerator for about 30 minutes or until firm.

6. Preheat the oven to 350°F. Line several cookie sheets with parchment paper or silicone baking mats.

7. Drop tablespoon-sized balls of dough onto cookie sheets about 2¹/₂ inches apart (these cookies will spread in the oven). Flatten with the palm of your hand. Sprinkle turbinado sugar over the tops.

8. Bake 10 to 12 minutes, rotating sheets halfway through. They should turn golden brown when they are done.

9. Cool sheets on wire racks for a few minutes before transferring cookies directly onto wire racks with a spatula to finish cooling.

Yield: About 2 dozen cookies

Storage:

Store in an airtight container for up to a week.

Variation:

Maple Glazed Cookies
Spread this simple maple glaze on top of cooled cookies for even more maple flavor.

In a small bowl, combine 2 cups confectioners' sugar, ¹/₃ cup maple syrup, and 1 tablespoon melted butter; add 3 to 4 tablespoons milk, enough get a spreadable consistency.

22. **MERINGUES**

General
Description:

*Meringues are light, airy puffs that are similar to **macarons**, but irregularly shaped.* They have a white, crackly shell and a very sweet, slightly chewy interior. Because meringues are usually made freeform, they often have a swirled or peaked appearance, depending on how the batter was dispensed onto the cookie sheet. The simplest method of making a meringue is to whip egg whites while slowly adding sugar until the white form stiff peaks. This type is known as French meringue, and it is usually used for making meringue cookies. Several desserts specifically call for meringues, such as baked Alaska, *pavolvas*, *oeufs à la neige*, and queen of puddings. Meringue cookies are a simple way to use this time-honored pastry technique.

| History: | The earliest known recipe for meringues was found in the recipe notebook of a Lady Elinor Fettiplace of Berkshire, England, dated 1604. Meringues became an integral part of European pastry and are now used in many European desserts. Making meringue cookies is an ideal way to use up old egg whites, especially since egg whites whip up better when they are aged. |

| Serving Suggestions: | Meringues are straightforwardly sweet due to the simplicity of the ingredients. Enhance the flavor by adding some ground almonds or hazelnuts to the sugar before whipping. Large piped meringues made with ground nuts are often used to make a dessert called *dacquoise*. A British dessert called Eton mess is made by layering small meringues with whipped cream and strawberries. |

| Baking Notes: | If you do not have old egg whites, try separating the egg whites a day before making the cookies and storing them in the refrigerator. Egg whites attain much more volume when whipped if they are at room temperature; be sure to give your whites adequate time to warm up. It may also take practice to determine how to add the sugar and how long to whip the egg whites. It is important not to add the sugar all at once or too soon, because it will prevent the whites from achieving volume. Wait until the whites have already formed peaks before adding the sugar, |

and always add in a steady stream. Do not overwhip, or the meringues will lose volume. Form and bake the meringues immediately after the batter is ready, to avoid having it deflate. Meringues are very sensitive to moisture in the air, so you may find that on humid days they take longer to bake. Meringues are ready when they feel dry and come off the cookie sheets easily. If they remain soft and sticky on a humid day, try leaving them in the turned-off oven overnight.

Recipe: **3 egg whites at room temperature**
$^1/_4$ teaspoon cream of tartar
I cup sugar

1.   **Preheat oven to 250°F. Line a cookie sheet with parchment paper.**

2.   **In a stand mixer with the whisk attachment, beat the egg whites on low-medium speed until foamy.**

3.   **Add cream of tartar and whisk on medium speed until soft peaks form.**

4.   **With the mixer running, add the sugar in a slow, steady stream and whisk until the meringue holds very stiff peaks.**

5.   **Dab a little meringue underneath the corners of the parchment paper on the cookie sheets to act as**

a glue keeping the paper in place. Fit a pastry bag
with a $^1/_2$-inch plain tip. Fill the pastry bag with
half of the meringue. Pipe 2-inch round mounds
of meringue onto the sheet. Refill the bag, and
continue piping the rest of the meringue in the
same manner.

6. Bake for 45 minutes to 1 hour, rotating sheets
halfway through. The meringues should not color,
but the outsides should become firm and dry. If
they do not seem to be done after 1 hour, turn off
the oven and leave them inside for another 20 to
30 minutes.

Yield: About 1 dozen cookies

Storage: Meringues should be eaten as soon as possible
            because they will absorb any moisture in the air and
            become sticky and soft.

23. ## MOLASSES SPICE COOKIES

General   *The molasses spice cookie is a close cousin to **gingersnaps***
Description: *and **gingerbread**—cookies that rely on ginger for the*
               main flavor punch. Molasses spice cookies are soft
               and chewy, unlike the crispier gingersnaps, and they
               get their unique flavor from a combination of spices
               and molasses. Molasses spice cookies have crinkly

tops and are usually covered with granulated sugar before baking, giving them a sparkly appearance. Sometimes they are also decorated with white icing, similar to gingerbread.

History:

Ginger has been used in ginger breads and cakes since the Middle Ages. When molasses was introduced to England in the 1600s, it became a cheap and popular substitute for sugar in recipes. Although many cookies made with molasses and ginger in America were based on recipes from the Old World, the molasses spice cookie appears to be a uniquely American distillation—its round shape and soft chewiness are much more typical of American baking.

Serving Suggestions:

The strong flavors and chewy texture of molasses spice cookies make them an ideal companion for a cold glass of milk. This cookie would also go nicely with some companion cookies, perhaps a sweeter chocolate cookie or a plainer nut cookie, to serve as an interesting contrast.

Baking Notes:

Be sure to use spices that are as fresh as possible, as much of the cookie flavor depends on them. The type of molasses used also affects the intensity and depth of flavor. Light and dark molasses are the most common types found in stores; both work well in this recipe.

Recipe: 2¹/₃ cups all-purpose flour
2 teaspoons baking soda
¹/₂ teaspoon salt
1 teaspoon ground cinnamon
1¹/₂ teaspoons ground ginger
¹/₂ teaspoon ground cloves
¹/₄ teaspoon ground allspice
³/₄ cup softened unsalted butter
¹/₂ cup dark brown sugar
¹/₂ cup sugar
1 egg
1 teaspoon vanilla extract
¹/₂ cup dark molasses
Extra sugar for rolling

 1. Sift flour, baking soda, salt, and spices into a bowl and set aside.

 2. In a stand mixer, cream butter and sugars on medium speed for several minutes until light and fluffy. Add egg and vanilla and mix until combined. Add molasses and mix until combined.

 3. Add flour mixture and mix on low just until incorporated.

 4. Cover dough and refrigerate for 15 to 20 minutes.

 5. Preheat the oven to 325°F. Line several cookie sheets

with parchment paper or silicone baking mats.

 6. Roll 1¹/₂-inch balls of dough in the reserved sugar. Place cookies on cookies sheets about 2 inches apart.

 7. Bake for 9 to 11 minutes, rotating cookie sheets halfway through. For crispy cookies, leave them in for another minute or two. Cool sheets on wire racks for about 5 minutes before transferring cookies directly onto wire racks with a spatula to finish cooling.

Yield: About 4 dozen cookies

Storage: Store in an airtight container for up to 2 weeks.

---

24. **NAZARETH SUGAR COOKIES**

General Description: *These soft and fluffy sugar cookies come from the town of Nazareth, Pennsylvania.* They are similar to **sugar cookies**, and they are also known as *Amish Sugar Cookies.* Pennsylvania state legislators recently closed a long debate over whether the Nazareth sugar cookie or the **chocolate chip cookie** ought to be named the official state cookie. Rep. Robert Thompson claimed that Pennsylvania leads all other states in

the production of processed chocolate but has no
ties to cane sugar. Other officials, led by Rep. Craig
Dally, claimed that Nazareth sugar cookies are an
important part of Pennsylvania heritage. Ultimately,
the Nazareth sugar cookie lost its bid, but it remains
an important part of Pennsylvania baking traditions.

History: Nazareth sugar cookies trace their origins to Europe.
Moravian German immigrants brought established
sugar cookie recipes and baking techniques to
America in the 1700s, resulting in **Moravian spice
cookies** and, in New England, **hermits**. In 1740, a
group of itinerant Moravian Protestants founded the
town of Nazareth in eastern Pennsylvania and pro-
ceeded to perfect these soft, delectable cookies.

Serving   Nazareth sugar cookies are strongly associated with
Suggestions: Christmas; however, they are suitable for any special
❄ ❄   occasion.

Baking Notes: This cookie has a very fluffy, cakey texture, so be sure
not to overmix the dough or overbake the cookies.

Recipe: **3¹/₂ cups all-purpose flour**
1 teaspoon baking soda
1 teaspoon cream of tartar
¹/₂ teaspoon salt
1 cup softened unsalted butter
2 cups sugar

2 teaspoons vanilla extract
1 cup sour cream
Extra sugar for sprinkling

1. Preheat oven to 375°F. Grease several cookie sheets.

2. Sift flour, baking soda, cream of tartar, and salt into a bowl and set aside.

3. In a stand mixer, cream butter and sugars on medium speed for several minutes until light and fluffy. Add eggs and vanilla and mix until combined.

4. Add the sour cream and mix until combined. Add the flour mixture and mix at low speed until combined.

5. Scoop dough into 1-inch balls and place onto cookie sheets about 3 inches apart.

6. Dip the bottom of a measuring cup in the extra sugar. Press down on each cookie with the measuring cup, slightly flattening the cookies and coating them with sugar.

7. Bake for 10–12 minutes or until the cookies start to brown, rotating cookie sheets halfway through. Cool sheets on wire racks for about 5 minutes before transferring cookies directly onto wire racks with a metal spatula to finish cooling.

Yield:	About 3 dozen cookies

Storage:	Store in an airtight container for up to 1 week.

25. **OATMEAL RAISIN COOKIES**

General
Description:
Oatmeal raisin cookies are some of the simplest cookies to bake, making them a great choice for beginning bakers. They are deep brown in color and have a craggy, bumpy surface from the oats and raisins mixed into the dough. The use of oats, along with their homey, rustic appearance, has given them a reputation as a comfort food as well a healthful food. They are one of the most popular cookies in the United States, along with **chocolate chip cookies** and Oreos (see **chocolate sandwich cookies**).

History:
Oatmeal cookies trace their ancestry to the oatcakes, or bannocks, made by the Scots and the British. The popularization of the modern oatmeal cookie can be attributed to Quaker Oats, which published a recipe for these treats on all their oat containers in the early 1900s and have enjoyed a connection with the cookie ever since.

Serving
Suggestions:
The easygoing flavor and chewy texture of this cookie make it very adaptable to additional

ingredients. Nuts like pecans or walnuts add crunch-iness and depth of flavor, while dried fruits like cran-berries give this classic cookie a holiday twist. Chocolate chips are a favorite substitute for raisins.

Baking Notes: Use old-fashioned rolled oats. Quick oats can be used as well; they are cut into small pieces to cook more quickly, so the cookies will have a less craggy texture. Note that steel-cut oats are much more coarsely cut and have not been steamed or flattened in the chopping process; their longer cooking time and stronger flavor make them better suited for oat-meal than cookies. Instant oats, too, should never be used for these cookies.

Recipe:
I¹/₂ cups all-purpose flour
³/₄ teaspoon baking soda
¹/₂ teaspoon salt
¹/₄ teaspoon ground nutmeg
¹/₂ teaspoon ground cinnamon
I cup softened unsalted butter
I cup light brown sugar
¹/₂ cup sugar
2 eggs
2 teaspoons vanilla extract
3 cups old-fashioned rolled oats
I¹/₂ cups raisins

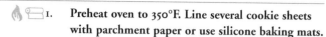 1. Preheat oven to 350°F. Line several cookie sheets with parchment paper or use silicone baking mats.

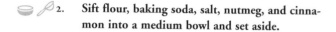 2. Sift flour, baking soda, salt, nutmeg, and cinnamon into a medium bowl and set aside.

3. In a stand mixer, cream butter and sugars on medium speed for several minutes until light and fluffy. Add eggs and vanilla and mix until combined.

4. Add flour mixture and mix on low just to combine. Stir in oats and raisins with a wooden spoon.

5. Scoop out tablespoon-sized balls of dough. Place on cookie sheets about 2 inches apart.

6. Bake for 12 to 14 minutes, rotating cookie sheets halfway through. The cookies are done when the edges are golden brown but the edges are still soft. Cool sheets on wire racks.

Yield: About 4 dozen cookies

Storage: Store in an airtight container for about 1 week.

26. **ORANGE DELIGHT COOKIES**

General
Description:

These beautiful light golden cookies are topped with tangy orange frosting. Oranges and citrus fruits have long been used in cookies. The citric acid—the bite—of these fruits plays off the rich, full flavor of the flour, butter, and sugar for a dynamic, layered taste.

History:

Most orange cookie recipes use orange zest, with the occasional tablespoon of orange juice here and there. In Italy, orange juice is used more prominently in delicious orange juice cookies that are traditionally dusted lightly with confectioners' sugar. Orange delights may trace their origins to Italian juice cookies.

Serving
Suggestions:

The light, delicate orange flavor of these cookies makes them well suited to the summer months, but they may also be enjoyed at Christmas.

Baking Notes:

Margarine tends to produce cookies that spread across the pan, so be sure to space cookies 2^{1}/2 inches apart on cookie sheets.

Recipe:

2 cups all-purpose flour
^{1}/2 teaspoon baking powder
^{1}/2 teaspoon baking soda
^{1}/2 teaspoon salt
^{2}/3 cup softened unsalted butter or margarine
^{3}/4 cup sugar

1 egg
2 tablespoons orange zest
1/2 cup orange juice

Orange frosting:
2¹/₂ tablespoons softened unsalted butter
1¹/₂ cups confectioners' sugar
2 tablespoons orange zest
1¹/₂ to 2 tablespoons orange juice

1. Preheat oven to 400°F.

2. Sift flour, baking powder, baking soda, and salt into a medium bowl and set aside.

3. In a stand mixer, cream butter and sugar on medium speed for several minutes until light and fluffy. Add the egg and orange zest and mix until combined. Add flour mixture and orange juice in three additions, alternating between the flour mixture and the juice.

4. Drop teaspoonfuls of dough onto an ungreased cookie sheet at least 2¹/₂ inches apart. Bake for 8–10 minutes. Remove and allow to cool on wire racks for at least 30 minutes before frosting.

5. For the frosting: In a stand mixer, cream butter and sugar at medium speed for several minutes

until light and fluffy. Add orange zest and juice,
and mix until smooth. Frost cooled cookies using
a rubber spatula.

Yield: About 3¹/₂ dozen cookies

Storage: Store in an airtight container for up to 1 week.

27. **PFEFFERNÜSSE**

General
Description:

Pfeffernüsse are small, firm German cookies. Pfeffernüsse
means "pepper nuts"; the cookies contain black pepper and ginger, giving them a spicy, robust flavor.
The cookies are rolled in confectioners' sugar or
frosted with white icing after baking, which provides
a sweet contrast to the complex piquancy of the
dough. Pfeffernüsse are usually made in small, round
balls, which, combined with the confectioners' sugar
coating, makes them resemble snowballs. Because of
their firmness, pfeffernüsse are often dipped in tea
or coffee before eating to soften them.

History: Many of the oldest pfeffernüsse recipes from the
medieval era do not call for black pepper. Spices like
pepper were rare and costly, and most people were
not able to obtain them easily. Bakers substituted
other spicy ingredients like ginger, but retained the

name of the cookie.

Serving
Suggestions:
田 ❄ ☕

Pfeffernüsse are classic European Christmas cookies that provide a counterpoint to some of the sweeter and more elaborate Christmas cookies.

Baking Notes:

The classic form of pfeffernüsse is a small round ball, but the dough adapts to many different forms. Instead of forming the dough into a disk, roll it into a log, chill in the refrigerator, and then cut off slices. Or roll out the chilled dough to about 1/2 inch thick, and use a cookie cutter to cut out shapes.

Recipe:

1/2 cup blanched almonds, toasted (walnuts can be substituted)
2 1/4 cups all-purpose flour
1/2 teaspoon baking powder
1/4 teaspoon baking soda
2 teaspoons ground cinnamon
1 teaspoon ground cardamom
1/2 teaspoon ground cloves
1/2 teaspoon ground ginger
1/2 teaspoon ground nutmeg
1/4 to 1/2 teaspoon black pepper
1/4 teaspoon ground anise seed
1/2 teaspoon salt
3/4 cup softened unsalted butter
1/2 cup dark brown sugar
1/4 cup sugar

2 egg yolks
$^1/_3$ cup dark molasses or corn syrup

Peppered powdered sugar:
$1^1/_2$ cups sifted confectioners' sugar
A few pinches of freshly cracked black pepper

1. Using a food processor, finely grind the almonds with 2 tablespoons of the flour. In a bowl, whisk together the ground almonds, the rest of the flour, baking powder, baking soda, spices, and salt, and set aside.

2. In a stand mixer, cream butter and sugars on medium-high speed for several minutes until light and fluffy.

3. Add egg yolks and mix until combined; add molasses and mix until combined.

4. With the mixer on low speed, add the flour mixture until just combined.

5. Flatten the dough into a disk, wrap well with plastic wrap, and refrigerate at least 3 hours, preferably overnight.

6. Preheat the oven to 350°F. Line several cookie sheets with parchment paper.

7. **Form dough into 1-inch balls. Place on cookie sheets about 1¹/₂ inches apart, and flatten the top of each. Bake for 10 to 12 minutes until the edges are golden brown, rotating sheets halfway through. Cool sheets on wire racks for a couple minutes before transferring cookies directly onto wire racks with a metal spatula to finish cooling.**

8. **For the peppered sugar: Combine the confectioners' sugar and pepper in a bowl. Roll cooled cookies in the sugar to coat completely.**

Yield: About 5 dozen cookies

Storage: Store in an airtight container for up to 2 weeks.

---

28.   **PIGNOLI COOKIES**

General Description: *Pignoli cookies are sweet Italian cookies made from almond paste and rolled in pine nuts.* Made from a combination of almond paste, sugar, confectioners' sugar, and egg whites, they are sweet, moist, and slightly chewy; the chewiness is offset by the crunchy nuttiness of the pine nuts. Pignoli cookies are popular in bakeries in southern Italy, especially around Christmas. Similar to the pignoli cookie is the *panellet*, a Catalan sweet that is made of ground almonds and mashed potato, and also covered in pine nuts. Panellets are made to celebrate All Saints' Day on November 1.

History:	Pine nuts are the seeds of the pine tree (*Pinaceae*) and an integral part of Mediterranean cuisine.
Serving Suggestions:	Pignoli cookies are an eye-catching addition to the holiday dessert table. You can dress them up even more by dipping them in melted chocolate. *Pinolate* are a well-known version of pignoli cookies, made with a combination of almond paste and hazelnut paste for a fusion of nutty flavors.
Baking Notes:	It is best to use almond paste rather than marzipan, since marzipan usually contains more sugar, which may affect the texture of the cookies. If your cookie dough seems to be on the soft side and has trouble keeping its shape in the oven, try adding a little flour (up to $1/4$ cup) to help it adhere. The longer you bake the cookies, the chewier they will become.
Recipe:	$1/2$ **cup sugar**
	$1/2$ **cup confectioners' sugar**
	$1/4$ **cup all-purpose flour**
	$1/8$ **teaspoon salt**
	$3/4$ **cup (8 oz) almond paste at room temperature**
	2 egg whites whisked well
	$1/2$ **cup pine nuts**

1. Sift sugars, flour, and salt into a medium bowl, and set aside.

2. In a stand mixer, beat almond paste on low speed for several minutes until it is broken up into small pea-size pieces.

3. Add half of the egg whites and continue mixing on low speed.

4. Add the flour mixture and mix until smooth and well combined. There might be some small pieces of almond paste that will not smooth out, but this will not affect the outcome of the cookie.

5. Add the remaining egg whites and continue mixing on low speed until well combined.

6. Cover dough and refrigerate for 1 hour.

7. Preheat the oven to 300°F. Line several cookie sheets with parchment paper (preferred) or use silicone baking mats.

8. Drop teaspoonfuls of dough onto sheets about 2 inches apart. Sprinkle the cookies with the pine nuts.

9. Bake 18 minutes or until light golden brown,

**rotating cookie sheets halfway through. Cool for
15 minutes on the cookie sheets, then peel the
cookies from the parchment paper, being careful
not to break them.**

Yield: About 2$\frac{1}{2}$ dozen cookies

Storage: Store in an airtight container for up to 2 weeks or
            freeze baked cookies in an airtight container for up
            to 1 month.

29a–b.   **PROFITEROLES**

General   *These light golden puffs sandwich a delicious cream
Description: filling and are often drizzled in chocolate or caramel.*
            Profiteroles are a French pastry made from *pâte à
            choux*, or choux pastry, a rich, eggy dough that bakes
            into a crisp, airy shell, and filled with any number of
            sweet fillings. The most common fillings are
            whipped cream, pastry cream, or ice cream. In
            America, the whipped cream–filled version is known
            as a cream puff. Profiteroles are also used to create
            the classic French dessert *croquembouche*, which
            translates to "crunchy in the mouth."

            To make a croquembouche, profiteroles are
            stacked on top of each other in a pyramid; the entire
            structure is then drizzled with caramel and decorated
            with whipped cream and spun sugar.

History:

The first version of *pâte à choux* was invented by Panterelli, one of the chefs Catherine de Medici brought with her to France when she married the future Henry II. A pastry chef named Avice modified the dough in 1760 and used it to make little buns that when baked resembled cabbages. The French word for cabbage being *choux*, this dough became known as *pâte à choux*. The legendary French chef Antoine Carême further refined the dough in the nineteenth century into its modern incarnation. Numerous classics of French pastry are made with *pâte à choux*, from profiteroles to éclairs to *religieueses* to Paris-Brest.

Serving
Suggestions:

Pile up profiteroles into a croquembouche for special occasions, or serve them as hors d'oeuvres for large parties or banquets. Profiteroles can be filled with almost anything; use different flavors of ice cream, or layer whipped cream and fresh fruit inside.

Baking Notes:

Pâte à choux is interesting because it is the only dough that is cooked before it is baked. The amount of moisture in the dough from the water, butter, and eggs all work to create steam, which makes the dough puff up in the oven. In order for the puffs to hold their shape, they must bake completely–the outsides should be golden brown and dry, and the insides just barely still moist. If the insides are still wet, the puffs will collapse after removal from the oven.

Return them to the oven and let them bake longer.

Recipe: **Pâte à Choux:**
1 cup all-purpose flour
1 teaspoon sugar
1/2 teaspoon salt
1/2 cup milk
5 tablespoons unsalted butter, cut into pieces
4 eggs (plus 1 if needed)
1 egg, beaten, for egg wash

Pastry cream filling:
1 cup milk
3 egg yolks
5 tablespoons sugar
2 tablespoons cornstarch
1 teaspoon vanilla extract

 1. Preheat oven to 400°F. Line several cookie sheets with parchment paper or silicone baking mats.

 2. Sift flour, sugar, and salt into a medium bowl and set aside.

3. Combine milk, butter, salt, and 1/2 cup of water in a medium saucepan and bring to a boil on medium heat.

 4. Add the flour mixture all at once. Reduce heat to low and stir constantly with a wooden spoon until mix-

ture forms a ball and pulls away from the sides of the pan, about 4–5 minutes.

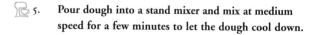 5. Pour dough into a stand mixer and mix at medium speed for a few minutes to let the dough cool down.

6. Add the eggs one at a time, letting each one incorporate fully before adding the next one. The dough should become smooth, shiny, and slightly sticky. If the batter looks stiff and dry, you can add a fifth egg.

7. Fit a pastry bag with a large plain tip. Fill pastry bag about half full with pâte à choux dough. Dab a little dough underneath the corners of the parchment paper on the cookie sheets to act as a glue to keep the paper in place.

8. Pipe rounds of dough onto the cookie sheets about 2 inches apart. Brush each round with a little egg wash.

9. Bake for 10 minutes, until the rounds have started to puff and rise. Reduce heat to 350°F, rotate the sheets, and bake for about 20 to 25 minutes more, when the puffs have turned golden brown.

10. Cool puffs completely on wire rack before filling.

11. For the pastry cream: In a medium saucepan, bring milk and 2 tablespoons of the sugar just to a simmer

over medium heat.

 12. Meanwhile, whisk together egg yolks and remaining sugar together in a medium bowl. Sift the cornstarch over the egg yolk mixture and whisk until incorporated.

 13. Pour half of the hot milk mixture into the egg yolk mixture, whisking constantly. Pour the egg yolk mixture back into the saucepan and return the stove.

 14. Cook the pastry cream over low heat until it comes to a boil, whisking constantly. Once it starts to thicken, whisk in the vanilla and cook for another 2 minutes.

 15. Strain pastry cream into a bowl, press a piece of plastic wrap against the surface, and refrigerate until it is completely cool.

 16. Once pâte à choux and pastry cream filling are both cooled, cut each profiterole in half and fill with pastry cream using a pastry bag or a small spatula.

Yield: About 3 dozen profiteroles

Storage: Store unfilled puffs in an airtight container for 4 days.
 If frozen, they can keep for up to 3 months. Pastry cream can be kept, refrigerated, for up to 4 days.

Variation: **_Profiteroles drizzled with caramel or chocolate_**
Melt chocolate or caramel (or both) and drizzle over
cream-filled profiteroles. Wait until ready to serve
before topping to prevent the profiteroles from getting soggy.

30. **ROCK CAKES**

General
Description:
*These humble cookie heaps may look rock-like, but they
are tastier than one might suspect.* When properly
baked, they have a crumbly, scone-like texture filled
with fruit and spices. Crisp on the outside and
crumbly on the inside, these cookies deserve a more
appetizing name.

History:
The rock cake is a traditional British biscuit similar
to the **ANZAC biscuit**. The sensible, hearty rock cake
has long been a teatime staple in the United Kingdom.

Serving
Suggestions:
These cookies must be served hot, and are best
slathered with jam and butter. Try replacing currants
with other fruit or 1 teaspoon orange zest.

Baking Notes:
Do not overbake, lest these cookies live up to their
name.

Recipe:
**1 3/4 cups all-purpose flour
2 teaspoons baking powder**

³/₄ cup sugar
1 egg
¹/₃ cup softened unsalted butter
3 tablespoons milk
¹/₂ cup currants

 1. Preheat oven to 350°F. Grease several cookie sheets.

 2. In a medium bowl, sift flour, baking powder, and sugar, and set aside. In a small bowl, beat egg until frothy.

 3. Using a rubber spatula, fold the butter into the flour mixture until roughly incorporated. Add egg and milk, and mix well until everything has been roughly incorporated. Add currants and continue to mix until a dough of medium stiffness has formed.

 4. Using a fork, scrape up enough dough to form craggy balls the size of a heaping tablespoon. Place 2¹/₂ inches apart on cookie sheets. Bake for 10–15 minutes or until golden and beginning to color at the edges, rotating cookie sheets halfway through. Remove from oven and cool slightly on wire racks before serving hot.

Yield: About 2¹/₂ dozen cookies

Storage: Rock cakes do not fare well in any sort of storage.
            They have a reputation for hardening into rocks
            overnight.

31.   **ROMANIAN (PRICOMIGDALE) COOKIES**

General   *An aromatic mélange of almond, rum, and toasted wal-*
Description: *nuts is the hallmark of these crispy, mocha-colored*
            cookies. These cookies are called *pricomigdale* in
            Romanian; *migdal* translates as "almond." They are
            extremely popular in Romania. They are baked year-
            round and served at church on holidays and birth-
            days, as well as at New Year's celebrations through-
            out southeastern Europe.

History: The cooking tradition of Romania reflects the coun-
            try's turbulent history of occupation and immigra-
            tion, and it is notable for its wide diversity of culi-
            nary influences. The Roman conquest of the region
            brought an influx of ingredients, such as almonds
            and honey. Romania's proximity to the Silk Road
            connecting Asia to Europe led to further diversity.

Serving   Serve Romanian almond cookies as an accompani-
Suggestion: ment to afternoon tea, espresso, or a hot mug of
    mocha. Serve them with champagne as a party treat
            on New Year's Eve.

Recipe:
1 cup sugar
1 cup softened unsalted butter
1 cup all-purpose flour
1 cup finely chopped walnuts
1 egg
1 teaspoon almond extract
1/2 teaspoon vanilla extract
2 teaspoons dark rum

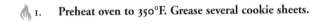

1. Preheat oven to 350°F. Grease several cookie sheets.

2. Using a stand mixer, cream together the sugar and butter at medium speed until light and fluffy.

3. In a small bowl, sift together flour and walnuts.

4. Add egg, almond extract, vanilla extract, and rum and mix until combined. Add flour mixture and mix until just combined.

5. Drop teaspoon-sized balls of dough onto sheets about 3 inches apart. Bake for 10 minutes or until slightly browned at edges, rotating cookie sheets halfway through.

Yield: About 3 dozen cookies

Storage: These cookies will keep for 1 week at room temperature in an airtight container.

32. **SESAME SEED COOKIES**

General
Description:

Thin, light, and crispy, sesame seed cookies from the American South are richly aromatic and delightfully crunchy from the sesame seeds scattered throughout. Also known as benne cookies or benne wafers, they can be made **tuile**-thin or as thick as a traditional cookie. Many forms of sesame seed cookies exist around the world, owing to the popularity of sesame seeds and their sweet, nutty flavor; benne cookies are one of the most well-known varieties.

History:

Sesame is used worldwide in a variety of foods, from hamburger bun topping to tahini. Sesame seeds were introduced to the South by slaves from West Africa, where sesame plants naturally grow. Africans called the seeds *benne* and considered them good luck. Benne cookies became popular in the South, where they are still made today, particularly in Charleston, South Carolina. Benne cookies are also made for Kwanzaa celebrations.

Serving
Suggestions:

Sesame seed cookies are wonderful with coffee or tea, or served with fruit as a light dessert.

Baking Notes:

Sesame seeds come in a variety of colors, from white to black. White seeds are typically used for sesame seed cookies, since they have a nutty flavor; black seeds have a stronger, more bitter taste. Toasting sesame seeds will bring out their flavor, but they tend to burn easily, so monitor them carefully: Spread out the seeds in an even layer on the cookie sheet and check the oven in 5 minute increments, shaking the pan to ensure even toasting. When the nuts become fragrant and lightly colored, they are done.

Recipe: **1 cup sesame seeds**
1 cup all-purpose flour
1/4 teaspoon baking soda
1/4 teaspoon salt
1 1/2 cups dark brown sugar
3/4 cup unsalted butter, melted
1 egg
1 teaspoon vanilla extract

 1. **Preheat oven to 375°F. Line a few cookie sheets with parchment paper or silicone baking mats.**

 2. **Spread sesame seeds in an even layer on an ungreased cookie sheet. Toast in the oven for 6 to 9 minutes until lightly colored and fragrant.**

 3. **Combine seeds with flour, baking soda, and salt in a bowl and set aside.**

 4. **Combine sugar, butter, egg, and vanilla in a medium bowl and stir together until fully combined.**

5. **Add the flour mixture and mix to combine.**

 6. **Drop dough by teaspoonfuls onto cookie sheets about 1¹/₂ inches apart.**

 7. **Bake for 6 to 8 minutes, rotating sheets halfway through. They should become golden brown. Cool sheets on wire racks for about 5 minutes before transferring cookies directly to racks with a metal spatula to finish cooling.**

Yield: About 3¹/₂ dozen cookies

Storage: Store in an airtight container for up to 1 week.

---

33. **SNICKERDOODLES**

General Description: *The snickerdoodle resembles the basic **sugar cookie**, except it has ground cinnamon added to the dough and each cookie is rolled in cinnamon sugar before baking.* Snickerdoodles have a speckled, crinkly surface; the flecks of cinnamon and the sugar form a crispy crust when baking. The interiors of snickerdoodles are usually soft and slightly chewy. Since there are no nuts, fruits, or other additions that might turn away the picky eater, snickerdoodles are almost universally popular.

History: The origin of the snickerdoodle is unclear. It appears to be an American creation, although the oldest recipes for cookies of that name are dated to the early 1900s. However, many recipes for snickerdoodle-like cookies have been found from colonial times. The word *snickerdoodle* is thought to be a nonsense term made up by American colonists. Other traditional cookies that might have been named this way include **jumbles**, plunkets, and kinkawoodles.

Serving Suggestions: Snickerdoodles are ideal cookies for children because of their mild, sweet flavor. Serve with a glass of milk and a variety of other homey cookies like **chocolate chip**, **molasses spice**, and **peanut butter**.

Recipe:
1¹/₃ cups all-purpose flour
¹/₂ teaspoon cream of tartar
¹/₂ teaspoon baking soda
¹/₈ teaspoon salt
¹/₂ cup softened unsalted butter
¹/₂ cup plus 2 tablespoons sugar
2 tablespoons light brown sugar
1 egg
1 teaspoon vanilla extract
¹/₄ cup sugar
4 teaspoons ground cinnamon

 1. **Preheat oven to 350°F. Grease several cookie sheets or line them with parchment paper.**

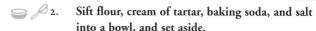

2. Sift flour, cream of tartar, baking soda, and salt into a bowl, and set aside.

3. In a stand mixer, cream butter and sugars on medium speed for several minutes until light and fluffy. Add egg and vanilla and mix until combined.

4. Add flour mixture in two additions, making sure the first addition is fully incorporated before adding the second.

5. Combine sugar and cinnamon in a small bowl.

6. Roll 1-inch balls of dough in the cinnamon-sugar mixture. Place on sheets about 2 inches apart. For a puffy cookie, leave balls as they are. For a flatter cookie, flatten each ball of dough slightly using the palm of your hand, to about 3/8 inch thick.

7. Bake cookies 9–10 minutes for chewy cookies or 12–13 minutes for crispy cookies, rotating sheets halfway through. Cool sheets on wire racks for a few minutes before transferring cookies directly onto wire racks with a spatula to finish cooling.

Yield: About 2 dozen cookies

Storage: Store in an airtight container for 4–5 days. These cookies may also be frozen for up to one month.

34. **SUGAR COOKIES**

See also **Sugar Cookies** (rolled), page 311–13.

General
Description: *The sugar cookie is a mainstay of the American cookie repertoire: sweet, simple, and infinitely versatile.* The cookie comes in two primary forms: a classic round shape similar to a chocolate chip cookie, and a rolled out dough that is cut with cookie cutters into different shapes and decorated, often with colored icing. The simpler round form is softer and has a lighter, fluffier texture common to drop cookies. It is usually light golden in color and has sugar sprinkled over the top to give it a sparkling appearance. The rolled version is firmer and crisper, which makes it ideal for decorating. Rolled sugar cookies are commonly decorated for the holidays and sometimes used as ornaments.

History: Sugar cane was found in ancient New Guinea and exported to India and other parts of Asia. Indians were the first to discover how to make sugar out of sugar cane juice around the year 350 AD. Arabs were instrumental in introducing sugar—as well as sweet cakes and cookies made with sugar—to Western Europe. Rolled and decorated sugar cookies seem to be a particularly North American tradition.

Serving
Suggestions: Sugar cookies go well with nearly everything due to their simple, straightforward flavor. It is easy to

modify the flavor; add a few teaspoons of spices or citrus zests to suit your taste.

Baking Notes:

If you are making drop-style sugar cookies, the simplest way to coat the balls of dough in sugar is to roll the balls with slightly damp hands. This will make the dough sticky enough for the sugar to adhere. If the dough is too cold and cracks while you are trying to roll it, let it sit for a few minutes to soften up before trying again. If you are cutting out different shapes, group cookies of similar size together on the cookie sheets so they will bake evenly.

Recipe:

3 cups all-purpose flour
1 teaspoon baking soda
1/4 teaspoon salt
1 cup softened unsalted butter
13/4 cups sugar
1/4 cup light brown sugar
2 eggs, beaten
2 teaspoons vanilla extract
Colored sugars, sparkling or sanding, for decoration

 1. **Sift flour, baking soda, and salt into a bowl and set aside.**

2. **In a stand mixer, cream butter and sugars on medium speed for several minutes until light and fluffy. Add the eggs and vanilla and mix until**

combined.

 3. With mixer on low speed, slowly add flour mixture and mix until combined.

 4. Cover dough and refrigerate for 45 minutes.

 5. Preheat oven to 325°F. Grease several cookie sheets or line them with parchment paper.

 6. Roll dough into 1-inch balls and place on cookie sheets about 2 inches apart. Slightly flatten dough balls with your hand. Sprinkle as desired with colored sugar.

 7. Bake for 9 to 10 minutes or until golden brown around the edges, rotating sheets halfway through. Cool sheets on wire racks for a couple minutes before transferring cookies directly onto wire racks with a spatula to finish cooling.

Yield: About 2 dozen cookies

Storage: Store in an airtight container for up to 1 week.

35. **TRIPLE CHOCOLATE COOKIES**

General
Description:
The triple chocolate cookie is a round, craggy cookie that boats a triple threat—melted chocolate, cocoa powder, and chocolate chips—resulting in a rich, intense cookie. Some recipes merely add cocoa powder to chocolate chip cookie dough, while others call for only chocolate powder and contain no chips. Although it resembles a chocolate chip cookie with more chocolate, the triple chocolate cookie is usually thicker and softer, with a fudgy center that is almost liquid when it comes out of the oven. Triple chocolate cookies are often considered synonymous with indulgence and decadence.

History:
The use of chocolate in American cookie recipes began around the early 1900s, when chocolate became more readily available to the general public. Chocolate was marketed as a healthful and nutritious food, which encouraged people to use it in their cooking.

Serving
Suggestions:

Serve these rich, chocolaty cookies warm with a cold glass of milk, or use them as a base for ice cream with toppings. Add a handful of white chocolate morsels to the batter to create a striking visual contrast, or add 2 teaspoons espresso powder to the flour to give the cookie a sophisticated edge.

Baking Notes: To preserve the soft, melting fudginess of triple chocolate cookies, it is important not to overbake them. The edges of the cooled cookies should just be firm and the centers should still be soft when you press them lightly.

Recipe:
1³/4 cups all-purpose flour
1/4 cup cocoa powder
1³/4 teaspoons baking powder
1/4 teaspoon salt
12 oz semisweet chocolate
1/2 cup softened unsalted butter
1¹/4 cups dark brown sugar
1/4 cup sugar
3 eggs
1¹/2 teaspoons vanilla extract
1 cup (6 oz) chocolate chips

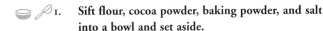

1. 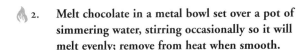 Sift flour, cocoa powder, baking powder, and salt into a bowl and set aside.

2. Melt chocolate in a metal bowl set over a pot of simmering water, stirring occasionally so it will melt evenly; remove from heat when smooth.

3. In a stand mixer, cream butter and sugars on medium speed for several minutes until light and fluffy. Add eggs and vanilla and mix until combined.

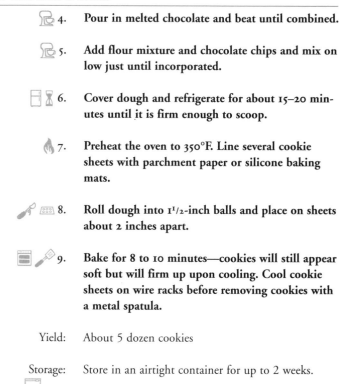

4. **Pour in melted chocolate and beat until combined.**

5. **Add flour mixture and chocolate chips and mix on low just until incorporated.**

6. **Cover dough and refrigerate for about 15–20 minutes until it is firm enough to scoop.**

7. **Preheat the oven to 350°F. Line several cookie sheets with parchment paper or silicone baking mats.**

8. **Roll dough into 1¹/₂-inch balls and place on sheets about 2 inches apart.**

9. **Bake for 8 to 10 minutes—cookies will still appear soft but will firm up upon cooling. Cool cookie sheets on wire racks before removing cookies with a metal spatula.**

Yield: About 5 dozen cookies

Storage: Store in an airtight container for up to 2 weeks.

36. 📷 **WHITE CHOCOLATE MACADAMIA COOKIES**

General
Description:

The contemporary combination of macadamia nuts, white chocolate, and coconut makes for a rich, deliciously indulgent cookie. This is one of many modern cookies that draw ingredients from across the globe: Macadamia trees originate in Australia, and native Australians have enjoyed the nuts for generations. Coconut palms grow in any tropical or subtropical environment. White chocolate is something of a misnomer—it is not actually chocolate but a combination of sugar, milk solids, and cocoa butter.

Serving
Suggestions:

When served with a variety of cookies, white chocolate macadamia nut cookies provide a nice contrast; they are distinct from more common cookies such as **chocolate chip**, **gingerbread**, or **sugar cookies** because they have an unusually high ratio of mix-ins to cookie batter.

Baking Notes:

Do not use dried coconut flakes, sweetened or unsweetened—the moist coconut is integral to this cookie. Be careful not to overbake to ensure a soft, fluffy texture.

Recipe:

1¹/₂ cups all-purpose flour
¹/₂ teaspoon baking powder
¹/₂ teaspoon baking soda
¹/₂ teaspoon salt

  3/4 cup softened unsalted butter
  3/4 cup sugar
  1/2 cup light brown sugar
  1 egg
  2 teaspoons vanilla extract
  1 cup (6 oz) white chocolate chips
  1 cup macadamia nuts
  1 cup shredded sweetened coconut

 1. Preheat the oven to 350°F. Line several cookie sheets with parchment paper or silicone baking mats.

 2. Sift the flour, baking powder, baking soda, and salt into a bowl and set aside.

 3. In a stand mixer, cream butter and sugars on medium speed for several minutes until light and fluffy. Add the egg and vanilla and mix until combined.

 4. Add the flour mixture, and mix on low speed just until combined; add the chocolate chips, macadamia nuts, and coconut and mix until evenly distributed.

 5. Roll dough into 1 1/2-inch balls and place on sheets about 2 inches apart.

 6. Bake for 8 to 10 minutes, rotating sheets halfway

through. When they're done baking, they should start turning golden brown but still be soft in the center. Do not overbake. Cool sheets on wire racks for a few minutes before transferring cookies directly onto wire racks with a spatula to finish cooling.

Yield: About 2 dozen cookies

Storage: Store in an airtight container for up to 1 week.

37a–b.

WHOOPIE PIES

General
Description:
A fluffy white filling is sandwiched between two deli-cious, soft chocolate cookies similar to devil's food cake. Whoopie pies are hugely popular in New England and Pennsylvania Dutch Country, as well as in Amish bakeries and roadside stands throughout the East Coast. In New England kitchens, the whoopie pie can be almost as big as a hamburger, while in Pennsylvania Dutch kitchens, it is a thick but mod-erately sized cookie.

History:
There is debate as to whether these cookie pies origi-nate in New England or the Pennsylvania Dutch communities of Lancaster county. In the 1800s and 1900s, entrepreneurs introduced recipes in an effort

to popularize their ingredients. In the 1930s, the Durkee-Mower Company popularized their Marshmallow Fluff by pairing it with a recipe for what was then called the Amish Whoopie Pie. Legend has it that whoopie pies got their name from the way Amish children would whoop when they found them packed in their school lunches.

Baking Notes: This recipe is written for the New England whoopie pie variety; for a smaller pie, portion out the dough with an ice cream or cookie scoop.

Recipe: **2 cups all-purpose flour**
1¹/₄ teaspoons baking soda
¹/₂ cup Dutch-process cocoa powder
1 teaspoon salt
1 cup light brown sugar
¹/₂ cup softened unsalted butter
1 egg
¹/₂ teaspoon vanilla extract
1 cup buttermilk

Filling:
¹/₂ cup softened unsalted butter
1¹/₂ cups confectioners' sugar
2 cups marshmallow cream (such as Marshmallow Fluff)
1¹/₂ teaspoon vanilla extract

1. Preheat oven to 350°F. Grease several cookie sheets.

 2. Sift together flour, baking soda, cocoa powder, and salt into a medium bowl, and set aside.

 3. In a stand mixer, cream butter and sugar on medium speed for several minutes until light and fluffy. Add egg and vanilla and mix until combined.

 4. Add the flour mixture and the buttermilk to the dough in 3 additions, alternating between wet and dry ingredients.

 5. Drop 1/4-cup mounds of dough 3 inches apart on cookie sheets. Bake for 12 minutes, rotating cookie sheets halfway through. Allow cookie sheets to cool for 5 minutes before moving cookies to wire racks with a metal spatula.

 6. For the filling: In a stand mixer, cream butter and confectioners' sugar at medium speed until light and fluffy. Add marshmallow cream and vanilla, decrease speed, and beat until smooth.

 7. Spread 1–2 tablespoons of filling across half of the cookies and place the other cookies on top. Then turn the spatula around the sides to even out the filling and keep it from spilling out.

Yield: About 1 dozen cookie sandwiches

Storage: The cookies can be kept in an airtight container for
             3 days, and the filling can be made up to 4 days in
             advance; however, they are best when eaten within a
             day or two of baking.

Variation: ***Peanut Butter Whoopie Pies***
             Sandwich this peanut butter filling between the
             chocolate cookies to make peanut butter whoopie pies.

             Peanut Butter Filling:
             3 tablespoons softened unsalted butter
             ¹/₂ cup creamy peanut butter
             3¹/₂ cups confectioners' sugar
             1 teaspoon vanilla extract
             ¹/₂ cup milk

             **Using a stand mixer, beat together the butter and
             peanut butter at medium speed until completely
             mixed. Add remaining ingredients and mix until
             light and fluffy.**

Bar Cookies

38a–b.

APPLE CRUMB BARS

General Description:

With the heady, spiced aroma of fresh apple pie and a generous layer of crumbled streusel, these bars are a delicious snack-sized version of the classic American dessert. Although they are similar to the ubiquitously popular apple pie, these bars are distinct in that they have less filling and more crunch in each bite.

History:

The first record of an apple pie recipe dates back to around 1390, in King Richard II's master chef Samuel Pegge's *The Forme of Cury*. In the 1300s, fruit pies contained no sugar, which was at that time a luxury good. The crust, known as the *coffin*, was simply a rough breadstuff used to contain the apple filling, rather than a flaky, delicious layer. By the 1500s, sugar was more readily available, and the modern apple pie began to take shape.

Serving Suggestions:

Serve these tasty bars à la mode, with a scoop of vanilla ice cream, or pair them with a hot cup of cider, spiked or nonalcoholic, before the fireplace.

Baking Notes:

Any firm, tart baking apple can be used in this recipe. Try Pippin, Cortland, or Gala. Add 1/2 cup cranberries for apple-cranberry crumb bars. The streusel can be made in a food processor or a stand mixer. In either case, be sure to stop when the mixture is still crumbly, with distinct pieces of butter; you do not want to get a solid ball of dough. The streusel is also a wonderful topping for muffins or quick breads. Just sprinkle some on top of the batter before baking.

Recipe: **Filling:**

3 large tart apples, such as Granny Smith (about 1³/4 lbs total)

3 tablespoons softened unsalted butter

¹/2 cup sugar

2 tablespoons lemon juice

2 tablespoons all-purpose flour

¹/4 teaspoon ground cinnamon

Crust:

2 cups all-purpose flour

1 teaspoon baking powder

¹/2 teaspoon salt

6 tablespoons softened unsalted butter

³/4 cup light brown sugar

1 egg

Streusel:

¹/2 cup sugar

²/3 cup plus 2 tablespoons all-purpose flour

¹/8 teaspoon salt

6 tablespoons cold unsalted butter, diced

$^1/_4$ cup chopped walnuts

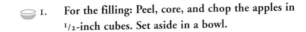

1. For the filling: Peel, core, and chop the apples in $^1/_2$-inch cubes. Set aside in a bowl.

2. Melt butter in a large sauté pan over medium heat. Add the apples and sauté for about 8 minutes until the apples are semi-soft.

3. Add sugar, lemon juice, flour, and cinnamon to the apples and stir to combine.

4. Cook until mixture begins to bubble, then turn heat to low and cook for another 3 minutes, stirring constantly. Transfer filling to a bowl and let cool while you make the crust.

5. For the crust: Line a 9 by 13 inch pan with aluminum foil, leaving enough to hang over the edge to form handles for removing bars after baking. Grease foil with cooking spray.

6. Whisk flour, baking powder, and salt together in a bowl and set aside.

7. In a stand mixer, cream butter and sugar together on medium speed for several minutes until light and fluffy. Add eggs and mix to combine.

8.   Add flour mixture and mix to combine.

9.   Pour the dough into the prepared pan and gently press into the bottom of the pan and about $1/4$ inch up the sides, making sure it is level. Set pan aside while you make the streusel.

10. Preheat oven to 350°F.

11. For the streusel: In a stand mixer, combine sugar, flour, and salt and mix to combine.

12. Add butter; mix until crumbly and the butter pieces are very small.

13. Add walnuts and mix just to combine.

14. Spread cooled apple filling evenly over the crust, leaving about $3/4$ inch between the pan sides and the filling.

15. Sprinkle the streusel evenly over the filling.

16. Bake for about 35 minutes until the top layer is golden.

17. Cool completely on wire rack before removing. Cut into 1-inch by 3-inch bars.

Yield: About 3 dozen bars

Storage:

Store lightly covered at room temperature for up to 4 days.

Variation:

Cherry Crumb Bars

Replace the apple filling with cherry filling: follow the apple filling recipe, substituting fresh or frozen pitted cherries for apples and omitting the cinnamon.

39. **BAKLAVA**

General Description:

Baklava is a pastry-like cookie made of several layers of crisp phyllo dough encasing a filling of nuts, sugar, and butter, and covered in a sweet honey syrup. Baklava is a popular dessert in the Mediterranean and the Middle East. Walnuts are the classic choice of nuts for baklava, and the honey syrup usually contains spices such as clove, cinnamon, and cardamom, giving the baklava a complex, multilayered flavor. Other recipes call for rosewater and pistachios, also common ingredients in the Middle East. Baklava is usually made in large sheets or rolls, then sliced into diamonds, squares, or triangles before baking.

History:

Baklava is popular throughout the Mediterranean and Middle East, and the earliest form can be traced back to the ancient Assyrians in the 8th century BC. This dessert was adopted by the Greeks, who modified it with their paper-thin sheets of phyllo dough, giving it the characteristic lightness and flakiness it is known for today.

Serving Suggestions:
♣ ⚙ ❄ ⊞

The filling for baklava can be varied to include different nuts such as almonds or pecans, or dried fruits such as raisins.

Baking Notes:

To prevent the phyllo sheets from drying out and cracking, leave them in the package until you are ready to use them. Don't worry if the sheets tear slightly while you are handling them; the other layers will help hold it together. Try to use a whole untorn sheet of phyllo for the top layer. Syrup may be made 1 day ahead and refrigerated. Although the amount of syrup may seem excessive when you are pouring it over the baklava, it will be absorbed over time.

Recipe:

Syrup:
1 cup sugar
1 cup water
1/2 cup honey
3 strips lemon peel
Juice of 1/2 lemon
3 strips orange peel
Juice of 1/2 orange
1 cinnamon stick
1/8 teaspoon ground cardamom

Baklava:

1 cup chopped almonds
1²/₃ cups chopped pistachios
¹/₃ cup light brown sugar
Heaping ¹/₂ teaspoon cinnamon
¹/₄ teaspoon ground cloves
¹/₈ teaspoon salt
1 pound phyllo dough (at least 21 sheets)
1 cup unsalted butter, melted

1. Prepare the syrup: Put all syrup ingredients in a medium saucepan, stir, and bring to a boil. Reduce heat to medium and simmer approximately 10 minutes until thickened. Remove from heat, strain out citrus peels and cinnamon stick, and set aside to cool.

2. Preheat oven to 350°F. Grease an 18 by 13 inch jelly roll pan.

3. Combine brown sugar, cinnamon, cloves, and salt in a medium bowl, and set aside.

4. Remove phyllo from package; use a sharp knife to trim it to the pan dimensions if necessary.

5. Pull out 7 sheets of phyllo. Keep any remaining dough covered at all times with a piece of waxed paper and a damp cloth.

6. Place one sheet of phyllo in the pan. Using a pastry brush, brush sheet with the melted butter; place a second sheet of phyllo on top and brush with butter. Repeat with the remaining five sheets.

7. Once you have buttered the top (7th) layer with butter, sprinkle it with half the nut mixture.

8. Repeat the process with another set of 7 phyllo layers, brushing melted butter between each layer, and topping the 7th layer with the remaining nut mixture.

9. Repeat with a third set of 7 layers of phyllo. Brush melted butter on top. Allow phyllo to set for approximately 10 minutes—this will make it easier to cut.

10. Using a very sharp paring knife, with the long side of the pan toward you, cut six horizontal strips. Make sure that the knife cuts all the way through down to the pan, and the six strips are completely separated from each other. Make diagonal cuts from top to bottom, cutting across the horizontal lines to create diamond shapes. Make cuts from $3/4$–$1^1/2$ inches wide, depending on desired size of baklava.

11. Bake until golden, 35–45 minutes. Pour the cooled syrup all over the hot baklava.

12. **Let baklava set for at least 1 hour before serving.**

Yield: About 4 to 7 dozen, depending on preferred size

Storage: Baklava will stay fresh for about 2 days, covered, at room temperature. Refrigerate baklava for up to 3 more days. Before serving, re-crisp in a 350°F oven.

40. **BISCOTTI**

General
Description:
Biscotti are dry, crisp cookies usually served with coffee, wine, or tea. They are meant to be dipped in a beverage to soften the texture before eating, hence their popularity in coffeeshops and teahouses. Biscotti dough is shaped into a long log and baked, then sliced into individual fingers and baked again to achieve their characteristic firmness. The shaping and slicing of the dough is what creates their thin, slightly curved shape. The unique two-step baking process is what gives biscotti their name, which means "twice-baked" in Italian. Biscotti are a cookie staple in Italy and have inspired twice-baked cookies in many other countries, including *zwieback* in Germany, *biscotte* in France, *paximadia* in Greece, *carquinyoles* in Spain, and **mandelbrot** throughout Eastern Europe.

History: Biscotti date back to Roman times, where they were conceived as a food for soldiers that would travel well and last a long time. Biscotti then were hard, dry biscuits meant more as a practical ration than a cookie. After the fall of the Roman empire, biscotti reemerged in Tuscany, where they were flavored with anise and almonds from the groves of Prato and served with Vin Santo, a famous local sweet wine, as a dessert. Today, this combination is still enjoyed in Tuscany, and the biscotti there are called *cantucci di Prato*. In the rest of Italy, biscotti are also called *cantucci*, and the word *biscotti* can be used to refer to any crisp cookie.

Serving
Suggestions:

Biscotti, naturally, are meant to be served with a drink, preferably a hot one. Biscotti dough is wonderfully adaptable to whatever additions you can dream up—all sorts of nuts, as well as dried fruits like raisins, currants, and cranberries. Dipping biscotti in melted chocolate makes a beautiful presentation. Because of their elegant shape, versatility, and excellent keeping qualities, biscotti are ideal holiday gifts.

Baking Notes:

The more well-formed your biscotti dough logs, the more shapely the resulting cookies will be. First, be sure to let the logs cool at least 15–20 minutes after the first bake before trying to slice them; otherwise you will smash and ruin the dough. When you slice the logs, use a sharp bread knife and a quick, steady stroke. Try to make all the sliced biscotti the same thickness so they will bake evenly. Be careful not to overbake biscotti; they should turn slightly golden, but they should not become deeply colored. This recipe uses cornmeal, which adds texture and crunch to biscotti. For a savory biscotti, see **Rosemary Parmesan Biscotti**.

Recipe:
1 3/4 cups all-purpose flour
1/4 cup cornmeal
1 cup sugar
1 teaspoon baking soda
1/4 teaspoon salt
2 eggs
Zest of 1 lemon
1 teaspoon vanilla extract
4 tablespoons unsalted butter, melted
3/4 cup pecans, toasted and roughly chopped

 1. Preheat oven to 350°F. Grease a cookie sheet or line with parchment paper.

 2. In a stand mixer, combine flour, cornmeal, sugar, baking soda, and salt. Add eggs, one at a time, and mix after each addition to fully incorporate. (The mixture will be very dry and crumbly.)

 3. Add zest, vanilla, and butter, mixing thoroughly until dough begins to form. It will not come together completely. Add pecans and mix just until evenly distributed.

4. Turn out dough onto a lightly floured surface. Use hands to form dough into one mass, then divide it into two equal pieces.

5. Roll each piece of dough into a log approximately $1^1/_2$ inches in diameter. Transfer each to cookie sheets, spacing them about 4–5 inches apart. Use palm of hand to flatten each log until they are 2–$2^1/_2$ inches across.

6. Bake for 20 minutes, rotating sheet halfway through. Remove from oven, and let biscotti logs rest on the cookie sheet for 20 minutes. Logs will still be slightly spongy to the touch, similar to a dense bread.

7. Lower the oven temperature to 250°F.

8. After 20 minutes, remove biscotti logs from pan and place on cutting board. Using a serrated knife, in one quick motion for each slice, cut log into $^1/_2$-inch slices. Return the slices, cut side up, to the cookie sheet. You can place the slices right next to each other, filling up the entire sheet, as the biscotti will no longer expand.

9. Bake biscotti for 40 minutes. Remove and cool on wire racks. Slices will be slightly soft while warm but will harden when cooled.

Yield: About 3 dozen biscotti

Storage: Store in an airtight container for up to 1 month.

41a–b. **BLONDIES**

General
Description:
*Blondies are a type of American cookie that resemble a
"blond" version of the brownie.* They are deep golden
in color and usually served in thick squares like
brownies. Blondies have a sweet, butterscotch flavor,
and they have a light, cakey texture. Blondies often
are studded with chocolate chips or chopped nuts,
such as pecans or walnuts. The difference between
brownies and blondies is more than simply the
presence or absence of chocolate. Blondies require
leaveners to achieve their fluffy texture, while most
fudgy-style brownies use none.

History: Recipes from colonial American times for cakes
using brown sugar or molasses may make them possible forerunners to the modern blondie. Interestingly,
the term "blondie" did not come into popular usage
until the 1970s, which may be why many people
believe that blondies were developed after brownies.

Serving
Suggestions:
Although the basic blondie recipe contains just
chocolate chips and pecans in the batter, many other

additions are possible. Butterscotch chips, peanut butter chips, toffee bits, and walnuts are among the most popular variations. Congo bars are another well known variation, where shredded sweetened coconut is added to the batter.

Baking Notes: The following recipe uses browned butter to increase the richness of the blondie. Light brown sugar is preferable to dark brown sugar, since it best emphasizes the sweet butterscotch flavor. Blondies taste best when they are still moist and soft, so take care not to overbake them. A toothpick inserted into the center of the blondies should come out with a few crumbs still on it.

Recipe: 1 cup unsalted butter
2 cups all-purpose flour
1 teaspoon baking powder
$^1/_2$ teaspoon salt
$1^1/_2$ cups light brown sugar
$^1/_2$ cup sugar
2 eggs
$1^1/_2$ teaspoons vanilla extract
$^2/_3$ cup chocolate chips
$^2/_3$ cup chopped pecans

 1. Preheat oven to 350°F. Line a 9 by 13 inch pan with aluminum foil, leaving enough to hang over the edge and act as handles to remove blondies

after baking. Grease foil.

 2. Brown the butter: In a small saucepan, melt butter over medium-high heat. Turn heat down to medium when the butter comes to a boil and begins to foam. Swirling the butter, continue heating until the liquid changes from a light yellow to a deep golden—be careful not to take it too far or it will burn. Remove butter from heat, and strain into a large mixing bowl.

 3. Sift flour, baking powder, and salt into a bowl and set aside.

 4. Add sugars to the melted butter and mix on medium-low speed to combine. Add eggs and vanilla and mix to combine. Add flour mixture and mix to combine.

 5. Add chocolate chips and pecans and mix to combine.

6. Pour the dough into prepared pan and spread evenly with a wet hand.

 7. Bake for 30 to 40 minutes (less for chewy blondies and more for firm ones).

8. **Cool blondies completely before removing from pan; using foil as handles, pull bars from the pan and place on a cutting board. Cut the long side five times, then cut four across the short side to create 20 squares.**

Yield: About 2 dozen

Storage: Store in an airtight container for up to 5 days.

Variation: ***Congo Bars***

Add 1 cup toasted sweetened flaked coconut to the batter when you add the chocolate chips and pecans.

42a–b. **BROWNIES**

General
Description: *Brownies are a type of American cookie characterized by their square, blocklike shape and rich chocolate flavor.* There are two common variations of brownies: fudgy brownies, which are dense, rich, and moist, and cakey brownies, which are lighter and fluffier and use leaveners to achieve their texture. Brownies, as their name indicates, are deep brown in color and often have a lighter brown, crackly top that develops during baking. Many brownie recipes often add walnuts to the batter, and a preference for nuts or no nuts is a source of debate among brownie enthusiasts.

Brownies sometimes are frosted on top with a thick chocolate icing. A very popular item on dessert menus is brownie à la mode, which pairs a brownie with a scoop of ice cream.

History:

The first recipes for brownies appeared in the 1906 edition of *The Boston Cooking-School Cookbook*, edited by Fannie Farmer, and the 1907 edition of *Lowney's Cook Book*, written by Maria Howard, one of Farmer's protégés. This likely coincides with the growing availability of chocolate to the general American public. Brownies started gaining popularity during the 1920s, and have been a mainstay of baking cookbooks ever since.

Serving Suggestions:

Brownies go well with a glass of milk. They can be served alone, or with some whipped cream or a scoop of vanilla ice cream. There are many ways to vary brownies; adding nuts or chocolate chips are popular options, while adding a few teaspoons of espresso powder will give them a more sophisticated flavor. For holidays, adding a teaspoon of peppermint extract to the batter is a subtle touch.

Baking Notes:

It is possible to vary the proportions of unsweetened and bittersweet/semisweet chocolates used, but it is best not to use semisweet chocolate alone; it will not give the brownies enough richness and depth of flavor. Be sure the chocolate and butter mixture has cooled to just warm before you add the other ingredients. For moist, fudgy brownies, it is important not to overbake the batter. If you insert a toothpick into the center, it should come out with some moist crumbs on it, and the brownie should look slightly wet in the center.

Recipe: ¹/₂ cup (3 ounces) unsweetened chocolate, chopped
6 tablespoons softened unsalted butter
1¹/₂ cups sugar
3 eggs at room temperature, beaten
1¹/₂ teaspoons vanilla extract
³/₄ cup all-purpose flour
¹/₂ teaspoon salt
³/₄ cup chopped nuts (optional)

 1. Preheat the oven to 325°F. If you are using a glass baking pan, decrease oven temperature to 300°F to avoid overbaking. Spray the bottom and sides of a 9-inch square cake pan with cooking spray.

 2. Melt chocolate and butter in a metal bowl set over a simmering pot of water on the stove, stirring the mixture periodically to ensure even melting.

 3. Whisk the sugar into the chocolate mixture. Allow the mixture to cool until warm.

 4. Whisk the eggs and vanilla extract into mixture

until smooth.

 5. **Add in the flour and the salt and combine with a wooden spoon until there are no lumps. Add the nuts (if desired) and mix well.**

 6. **Pour mixture into prepared pan and level with an offset spatula.**

 7. **Bake for 20–24 minutes, rotating pan halfway through; be careful not to overbake. Cool completely on wire rack before cutting into squares.**

Yield: About 16 brownies

Storage: Store in an airtight container for up to 4 days or freeze for 2 weeks in an airtight container.

Variations: ***Frosted Brownies***

If you like your brownies with a layer of creamy frosting, here is an easy ganache. Chop 1 cup (6 oz) of semisweet chocolate and place in a bowl. Heat 1/2 cup of heavy cream in a saucepan over medium heat until it just starts to bubble. Pour the cream over the chocolate, let sit for about a minute, and then stir to combine. If the chocolate does not melt completely, place the bowl over a pot of simmering water on the stove and heat until it is smooth and melted. Let the mixture cool slightly before pouring it over the pan of cooled brownies. Let brownies stand for about an hour for the ganache to set before cutting.

Rocky Road Brownies

Up the decadence factor of your brownies: While the brownies are baking, combine 1¹/₂ cups miniature marshmallows with 1 cup chopped pecans or walnuts. When the brownies are done, pull them out and cover with the marshmallow topping. Turn on the broiler and immediately return the brownies to the oven. Broil for 2–3 minutes until the topping melts. Let cool on wire rack before serving. Drizzle the top with chocolate or caramel sauce before serving.

43. **FIG BARS**

General Description:
Fig bars are soft, cakelike cookies made of a sweet dough wrapped around a fig filling, which is then cut into square or rectangular bars. The most well-known form of the fig bar is the Fig Newton, manufactured by Nabisco. A common misconception is that Fig Newtons were named after Sir Issac Newton; the cookies were actually named after Newton, Massachusetts, a town near the bakery where they were first popularized. Much of the mystique surrounding Fig Newtons concerns how the cookies are assembled. The commercial process of making Fig Newtons cannot be duplicated in the home kitchen,

but a simple fruit-filled bar cookie in their style can be easily made.

History:

The original fig bar is credited to Charles Roser of Ohio, who sold his creation in 1891 to Kennedy Biscuit Works, which would later become part of Nabisco. There is debate over whether Roser came up with just the recipe or also the machine that made mass production of the cookie possible. Nabisco claims that James Henry Mitchell, a Philadelphia inventor, came up with the system that allowed for rapid assembly of the Fig Newtons. Because Kennedy Biscuit Works and many other small bakeries were absorbed into the single company that would become Nabisco, it is difficult to determine the specific origins of many cookies that became part of Nabisco's product line. Today, Fig Newtons are one of Nabisco's best-selling products, and they come in a variety of flavors.

Serving Suggestions:

Fig bars, with their lightly sweet brown sugar dough serving as a backdrop for the fruit filling, are ideal for those who prefer their cookies less sweet and sugary. It is simple to substitute a variety of fruits in the filling. They make excellent lunchtime or afternoon treats for kids.

Baking Notes:

Parchment paper is very helpful when forming the cookie log, allowing you to work and fold the dough

more smoothly. When sealing the edges of the
dough to form the seam, be sure to press firmly to
smooth out the dough and prevent a thick layer
from forming. The recipe below is partially based on
date-nut pinwheels, another classic American cookie;
dates make an excellent substitution for figs in the
filling.

Recipe: **2 cups plus 2 tablespoons all-purpose flour**
¹/₂ teaspoon baking soda
¹/₄ teaspoon salt
¹/₂ cup softened unsalted butter
1 cup light brown sugar
1 egg
³/₄ teaspoon vanilla extract
1 teaspoon orange zest

Filling:
1¹/₄ cups dried figs, chopped
1 tablespoon sugar

 1.   **Sift flour, baking soda, and salt into a bowl and set aside.**

 2.   **In a stand mixer, cream butter and brown sugar on medium speed for several minutes until light and fluffy. Add the eggs, vanilla, and orange zest and mix until combined.**

3. Add flour mixture and mix on low speed just until combined.

4. Turn dough out onto a piece of plastic wrap. Flatten into a disk, wrap tightly, and chill in refrigerator for 1 hour. Meanwhile, make the filling.

5. Combine figs, sugar, and 1 cup of water in a small saucepan. Bring mixture to a boil. Reduce heat and cook until it reaches a jammy consistency. Set aside and let cool.

6. Roll out half of the dough on a lightly floured surface into an 8 by 13 by 1/8-inch thick rectangle. Transfer dough to a piece of parchment paper and trim to 7 by 12 inches.

7. Spread half the filling down the middle long third of the dough.

8. Fold the top third of the dough over the filling, using the parchment paper to help guide your fold.

9. Fold the bottom third of the dough over the filling, overlapping the top third by about 3/4 inch. Press dough together to seal seam.

10. Flip cookie log over onto the seam side and chill in refrigerator for 20 minutes.

11. Repeat with the second half of dough and rest of filling.

 12. Preheat oven to 375°F. Line a cookie sheet with parchment paper.

13. Place both logs on sheet about 4 inches apart.

 14. Bake for 20 to 23 minutes, until the logs are golden brown and firm to the touch. Cool completely on wire rack before cutting.

15. Using a serrated knife, cut log into 1^1/$_2$-inch wide slices.

Yield: About 16 slices

Storage: Store in an airtight container for up to 1 week.

44. **GRANOLA BARS**

General Description: *The granola bar is a hearty bar cookie made with granola cereal or homemade granola combined with brown sugar and honey.* It is usually formed in a compact, thin rectangle and has a firm composition that does not crumble easily, making it ideal for transportation. The bar can contain any number of additions, including dried fruit or nuts; the typically healthful nature of these additions, along with granola's wholesome reputation, leads many to consider granola bars a healthy snack. Granola bars can be crispy, or moist and chewy; they have a rustic, lightly sweet flavor from the toasted oats and brown sugar, combined with the crunch of nuts.

History: The term *granola* was coined in the late-1800s in America to describe whole grains cooked until crispy. Originally, this term was used mainly at hospitals to make plain grains more palatable to patients. Later, fruits and nuts were added to granola to make it more appealing to the public, and it was marketed as a health food. Granola bars were first created by Stanley Mason to make a more portable form of the loose granola.

Serving Suggestions: Granola bars can be packed with a variety of extras, from healthy to indulgent. You can add different nuts like pecans, walnuts, or almonds, or dried fruits like dates, raisins, and cranberries. Adding chocolate chips or shredded coconut pushes these cookies into the realm of sweet treat.

Baking Notes: If you like your granola bars on the drier, crunchier side, leave the bars in the oven for a few minutes longer.

Recipe: 2¹/₄ cups instant oats
              ¹/₂ cup maple syrup
              ¹/₄ cup honey
              ¹/₄ cup sunflower seeds
              ¹/₂ cup chopped almonds
              ¹/₂ teaspoon salt
              2 tablespoons light brown sugar

1. Preheat oven to 325°F. Coat a 9 by 13 inch baking pan with nonstick spray.

2. Spread oats on an ungreased cookie sheet and toast in the oven for 5–8 minutes, until lightly browned. Remove and put in a large mixing bowl.

3. In a small saucepan, heat maple syrup and honey over low heat, stirring occasionally, until mixture is thin.

4. Add syrup and honey to oats, and mix to combine.

5. Add remaining ingredients and mix to combine. The mixture will be crumbly. If it seems especially dry, add extra syrup.

6. Spread mixture into pan. Wet hands with water (to prevent sticking) and pat granola down tightly and evenly.

7. Bake for 25 minutes, rotating pan halfway through.

Let cool for 10 minutes. Loosen around edges with an offset spatula or butter knife. When granola has cooled slightly but is still warm, turn out onto cutting board. Using a chef's or serrated knife, trim granola piece to an 8 by 12 inch rectangle. Cut along the long side to create 6 strips that are 2 inches wide. Cut each strip in half to make 12 bars, 2 by 4 inches each.

8. If you prefer chewy granola, simply allow the bars to cool. If you prefer a crunchy version, return bars to oven on a cookie sheet for 10–15 minutes until they turn slightly golden. Do not overbake.

Yield: About 1 dozen bars

Storage: Store in an airtight container for up to 1 week.

---

45. **LEMON BARS**

General Description: *Lemon bars, sometimes called lemon squares, are a type of American cookie consisting of a soft lemon filling baked atop a crisp, buttery, shortbread-like crust.* Often the top is sprinkled with confectioners' sugar before serving. The crust is generally a simple buttery dough that is pressed into the pan. The lemon filling is a curd made with sugar, eggs, lemon juice, and lemon zest that bakes into a creamy, just firm, sunny yellow layer. The best lemon bars are a combination of citrus tartness and buttery sweetness.

History:

Lemon bars became a popular dessert in America in the 1970s after recipes for them appeared in Betty Crocker cookbooks and Maida Hatter's dessert cookbook. Interestingly, lemon meringue pie, which shares some similarities with lemon bars, was already commonly found in cookbooks by the early 19th century. Lemons are believed to have originated in India, although they are now grown in many places around the world.

Serving
Suggestions:

Try substituting lime or orange juice for lemon juice to give the bars a different citrus tanginess. Or use Meyer lemons to give the bars a sweeter, mellower flavor. For an exotic twist, try yuzu juice; this Asian citrus has a flavor reminiscent of lemon and grapefruit mixed together.

Baking Notes:

Choose lemons that have bright, vibrant yellow color and feel heavy in the hand. When you zest the lemons, be sure not to cut too deep, and take out the white inner membrane; this is the pith, which is quite bitter. Be sure that the crust is completely baked before you add in the filling, otherwise you may end up with a soggy one. If you are having difficulty slicing the bars neatly, let them stand for a few hours to firm up.

Recipe: **Crust:**
2 cups all-purpose flour
$1/2$ cup confectioners' sugar
$1/4$ teaspoon salt
1 cup cold unsalted butter, cut in $1/2$-inch pieces

Filling:
4 eggs
2 cups sugar
$1^1/2$ teaspoons lemon zest
$1/2$ cup fresh, strained lemon juice
$1/4$ cup all-purpose flour
1 teaspoon baking powder
About $1/4$ cup confectioners' sugar, for dusting

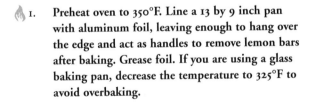

1. Preheat oven to 350°F. Line a 13 by 9 inch pan with aluminum foil, leaving enough to hang over the edge and act as handles to remove lemon bars after baking. Grease foil. If you are using a glass baking pan, decrease the temperature to 325°F to avoid overbaking.

2. In a stand mixer, mix the crust ingredients on low speed until a coarse meal is formed. (This can also be done in a food processor.)

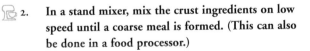

3. Pour the dough into the prepared pan and gently press into the bottom, making sure it is level.

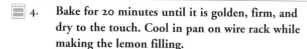

4. Bake for 20 minutes until it is golden, firm, and dry to the touch. Cool in pan on wire rack while making the lemon filling.

5. In a mixing bowl, whisk the eggs and sugar together until well combined. Whisking by hand allows for a richer filling; a mixer will incorporate too much air.

6. Add the lemon zest and lemon juice to the mixture and whisk well. Add the flour and baking powder and whisk well for about a minute.

7. Pour mixture on top of the cooled crust.

8. Bake for 20 to 25 minutes, rotating pan halfway through, until filling is almost set and jiggles just slightly when the pan is moved. Cool completely on a wire rack before cutting.

9. Using a sharp chef's knife, cut the long side into five strips, then cut four across the short side to create 20 squares.

10. Dust top of lemon bars with sifted confectioners' sugar.

Yield: About 2 dozen

Storage:

Store in an airtight container for up to 4 days at room temperature or for up to 10 days in the refrigerator. Bring to room temperature before serving.

46.

MAGIC COOKIE BARS

General
Description:

These rich bars are popular across the United States and boast an easy-to-bake mélange of seven layers of ingredients. Also known as *American 7-layer bars* or *Hello Dollies*, these attractive bars are relatively recent innovations. One of the key ingredients, sweetened condensed milk, was not invented until 1856 by the famed Texan inventor Gail Borden. Magic bars also demarcate the growing access and affordability of a greater variety of ingredients in the following decades, making use of crumbled graham crackers, coconut, pecans, and chocolate and butterscotch chips.

Serving
Suggestions:

Magic bars have long been a favorite at bake sales and pot lucks. Because these bars are made almost entirely of mix-ins—no flour, eggs, or leaveners— the recipe is very open to experimentation.

Baking Notes:

Try substituting traditional graham crackers with flavored crackers or crumbled Oreos. Many recipes cut the butterscotch and stick with chocolate chips, white chocolate chips, or M&Ms.

Recipe: ¹/₂ cup unsalted butter, melted
1¹/₃ cups crumbled graham cracker
1¹/₂ cups sweetened flaked coconut
¹/₂ cup (6 oz) semisweet chocolate chips
¹/₂ cup (6 oz) butterscotch chips
1 cup sliced pecans or other nuts
1 can (14 oz) sweetened condensed milk

 1. Preheat oven to 350°F.

2. Pour melted butter into a 9 by 9 inch baking pan and spread evenly.

3. Pour graham cracker crumbs across the bottom and gently tamp down with a rubber spatula.

4. Drizzle condensed milk over the crumbs.

5. Evenly sprinkle coconut, chocolate chips, butterscotch chips, and nuts across the pan.

6. Bake for 25–30 minutes. Remove from oven and cool completely before cutting into 2 by 2 inch bars with a sharp knife.

Yield: About 2 dozen bars

Storage: Store in a refrigerated airtight container for up to 1 week; their texture crumbles if frozen.

Color Plates

Icon Key

SEASON

spring	summer	fall	winter

TOOLS

stand mixer	bowl	blender or food processor	brush

cookie scoop	microplane zester	rubber spatula	metal spatula

pastry bag	whisk	sifter	cutter

cookie cutters	spoon	parchment paper	paper towels

TOOLS (continued)		
cookie sheet	heat	oven

STORAGE

sealed plastic bag	refrigerator	freezer	airtight container

SERVING SUGGESTIONS

gift	coffee or tea	milk

INGREDIENTS

mix-ins	chocolate kiss	sprinkles

MISCELLANEOUS

time	caution	heart healthy	photograph

1. amaretti

2a. Amish puffs
2b. chocolate chip puffs

3a. ANZAC biscuits
3b. trail mix biscuits

4. banana chocolate chip

5. **black and white cookies**

6. **brandy snaps**

7a. **Chickasaw pumpkin cookies**
b. with chocolate chips

8a. **Chinese almond cookies**
8b. **Chinese walnut cookies**

9a. **chocolate chip**

9b. **chocolate chip ice cream sandwiches**

10. **chocolate crinkles**

11. **chocolate espresso cookies**

12. **coconut macaroons**

13. **cowboy cookies**

14. **Florentines**

15. **French macarons**

16. **hermits**

17. **jumbles**

18. **lace cookies**

a

b

19a. **lavender orange puffs**
19b. **lavender glazed puffs**

20. **mahón cheese puffs**

a

b

21a. **maple cookies**
21b. **maple glazed cookies**

22. **meringues**

23. **molasses spice cookies**

24. **Nazareth sugar cookies**

25. **oatmeal raisin cookies**

26. **orange delight cookies**

27. **pfeffernüsse**

28. pignoli

29a. profiteroles

29b. profiteroles
drizzled in caramel and chocolate

30. rock cakes

31. **Romanian almond cookies**

32. **sesame seed cookies**

33. **snickerdoodles**

34. **sugar cookies**

35. **triple chocolate cookies**

36. **white chocolate macadamia cookies**

37a. **whoopie pies**

37b. **peanut butter whoopie pies**

38a. **apple crumb bars**

38b. **cherry crumb bars**

39. **baklava**

40. **biscotti**

41a. **blondies**
41b. **congo bars**

42a. **brownies**
42b. **frosted brownies**

43. **fig bars**

44. **granola bars**

45. **lemon bars**

46. **magic cookie bars**

47. **Mandelbrot**

48. **Nanaimo bars**

49a. pecan pie bars
49b. chocolate pecan pie bars

50. rainbow cookies

51. rosemary parmesan biscotti

52. turtle bars

53. financiers

54. fortune cookies

55. gingersnaps

56. Greek butter cookies

57. **Greek Easter cookies**

58. **Greek honey macaroons**

59. **Indonesian pineapple cookies**

60. **Italian Easter cookies**

61a. jam thumbprints

61b. buttercream thumbprints

62. ladyfingers

63. lebkuchen

64a. **madeleines**
64b. **jam-piped madeleines**

65. **peanut butter blossoms**

66a. **peanut butter cookies**
66b. chocolate peanut butter sandwiches

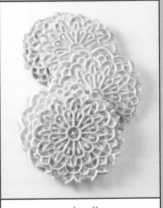

67. **pizzelles**

68. **red wine cookies**

69. **Russian tea cakes**

70. **speculaas**

71. **springerle**

72a. **spritz cookies**

72b. **chocolate spritz cookies**

73. **stroopwafels**

74. **tuiles**

75. TV snacks

76. Viennese almond crescents

77. alfajores

78. Algerian almond tarts

79. **animal crackers**

80. **biscochitos**

81a. chocolate sandwich cookies
81b. peppermint chocolate sandwiches

82. **gingerbread**

83. **green tea cookies**

84. **assorted hamantaschen**

85. **Indian almond cookies**

86. **Linzer cookies**

87. **Moravian spice cookies**

88. **palmiers**

89. **pecan sandies**

90a. **harlequin cookies**

90b. **bowtie cookies**

90c. **pinwheel cookies**

90d. **striped cookies**

90e. **checkerboard cookies**

91. **pistachio almond cookies**

92a. **rolled rugelach**

92b. **crescent apricot rugelach**

93. **sablés**

94. **sea salt and white peppercorn coins**

95a. **shortbread**

95b. **shortbread dipped in chocolate**

96. **sour cream biscuits**

97. **South African spiced wine cookies**

98. **stained glass cookies**

99. **iced sugar cookies**

100. **Swedish sandwich cookies**

47. **MANDELBROT**

General
Description:

*Mandelbrot is a thin crisp cookie that was adapted from Italian **biscotti** by Eastern European Jews.* In the Ukraine it is called *kamishbrot*. Mandelbrot has the same slightly curved shape as biscotti; the main difference between the two is that mandelbrot is usually made with oil, resulting in a tender cookie. Many modern mandelbrot recipes use butter, but traditional recipes call for oil in order to keep them *pareve* (non-dairy). The higher fat content means mandelbrot does not need to be dipped in a beverage; it will likely become soggy or crumble if left in liquid too long. However, it is still a popular accompaniment for tea or coffee. Mandelbrot is served at Jewish holidays, especially Passover.

History:

Mandelbrot means "almond bread" in Yiddish. There are a few theories about its origin. One is that biscotti spread with the Roman legions through medieval Eastern Europe, and the cookie was adapted by Jews living there. Another theory is that a large number of Jews settled in Piedmont, Italy, starting in the 15th century, and they picked up the recipe there.

Serving
Suggestions:

Mandelbrot is a good compromise for those who find biscotti too hard and austere, but softer drop-style cookies too sweet and light. Because of its tender,

soft texture, mandelbrot is particularly suited to
sweet additions like chocolate chips, dried cherries,
and pecans. Dipped in chocolate, it makes a beautiful
gift. Mandelbrot is traditionally served with hot tea.

Baking Notes: See the entry on **biscotti** for tips on shaping and
slicing the logs of mandelbrot dough. As with biscotti,
mandelbrot will continue to firm up after it has
been removed from the oven, so do not overbake it.

Recipe: **2¹/₂ cups all-purpose flour**
¹/₄ teaspoon baking soda
1 teaspoon baking powder
¹/₄ teaspoon salt
4 tablespoons softened unsalted butter
¹/₂ cup plus 2 tablespoons sugar
4¹/₂ teaspoons vegetable oil
2 eggs
³/₄ teaspoon fresh lemon juice
¹/₂ teaspoon vanilla extract
¹/₄ teaspoon almond extract
¹/₂ cup chocolate chips
¹/₂ cup chopped almonds

 **1.   Preheat oven to 350°F. Grease a cookie sheet or
line with parchment paper.**

 **2.   Sift flour, baking soda, baking powder, and salt
into a bowl and set aside.**

3.   In a stand mixer, cream butter and sugar on medium speed for several minutes until light and fluffy. Add oil and mix to combine.

4.   Add eggs, one at a time, and mix until fully incorporated. Add lemon juice and extracts.

5.   Add flour mixture in two additions. Mix just until combined. Add chocolate chips and almonds and mix to combine.

6.   Turn out dough onto lightly floured work surface. Form dough into one mass, then divide into two equal pieces.

7.   Roll each piece of dough into a log about 1 1/2 inches in diameter. Transfer each to the cookie sheet, spacing them about 4–5 inches apart. Use palm of hand to flatten each log until it is about 1/2 inch thick.

8.   Bake for 20 minutes, rotating sheet halfway through. Let mandelbrot logs rest on a cookie sheet for 20 minutes. Logs will still be slightly spongy to the touch, similar to a dense bread.

9.   Lower the oven temperature to 250°F.

10. **After 20 minutes, remove mandelbrot logs from sheet and place on a cutting board. Using a serrated knife, in one quick motion for each slice, cut log into ¹/₂-inch slices. Return the slices, cut side up, to the cookie sheet. You can place the slices right next to each other, filling up the entire sheet, as the mandelbrot will no longer expand.**

 11. **Return sheet to the oven and bake cookies for 40 minutes. Remove and let cool.**

Yield: About 4 dozen cookies

Storage: Store in airtight container for up to 10 days. These
       cookies are also excellent frozen and will stay fresh
              for up to 6 weeks.

48.   **NANAIMO BARS**

General   *These elegant three-layer bars are famous for their iconic*
Description: *status in their namesake city in British Columbia,*
              Canada. A coconut, chocolate, and graham cracker
              crumb base are layered with a light, creamy pudding
              and topped with a smooth chocolate, then cut into
              bar cookies. Nanaimo, pronounced *na-NY-mo*, refers
              to a confederacy of five Salish Native American
              bands that wintered in a collective village where the
              city of Nanaimo stands today.

History:	Reportedly, these cookies were invented and named by an anonymous housewife who titled a recipe she submitted to a magazine after her hometown. There are various stories surrounding this cookie's origins, and some even call this bar the *New York Slice*. In 1986, the city of Nanaimo held a four-week contest in search of the ultimate Nanaimo bars, and nearly 100 different recipes were submitted. In the end, Joyce Hardcastle's entry was declared victor, and her version is now considered the official recipe. The city is so proud of the bar that the town's mascot is a giant Nanaimo bar named "Nanaimo Barney."
Serving Suggestions:	These rich, attractive bars are often served in bite-sized pieces in coffee shops across North America.
Baking Notes:	This recipe is an adaptation of Joyce Hardcastle's Ultimate Nanaimo Bar recipe. To make mint Nanaimo bars, add 1 teaspoon mint extract and 2–3 drops of green food coloring to the custard layer and replace the chocolate in the third layer with mint chocolate. Try different kinds of nuts in your first layer.
Recipe:	**First layer:** $^1/_2$ **cup softened unsalted butter** $^1/_4$ **cup sugar** $4^1/_2$ **tablespoons cocoa powder**

1 egg, beaten
1 teaspoon vanilla extract
1¹/₂ cups finely crumbled graham cracker crumbs
1 cup sweetened flaked coconut
¹/₂ cup finely chopped walnuts

Second layer:
¹/₄ cup softened unsalted butter
2 tablespoons instant vanilla pudding mix
3¹/₂ tablespoons milk
2 cups confectioners' sugar

Third layer:
4 oz semisweet chocolate
1¹/₂ tablespoons softened unsalted butter

 1. In a metal bowl over a pot of simmering water, stir together the butter, sugar, cocoa, egg, and vanilla, then remove from heat.

 2. In a medium bowl, stir together graham cracker crumbs, coconut, and walnuts.

 3. Gradually stir the chocolate mixture into the crumb mixture. Add the egg and mix until combined. Press mixture into a 9 by 9 inch baking pan, and refrigerate until firm.

 4. In a stand mixer, beat butter, vanilla pudding mix,

milk, and confectioners' sugar at medium speed
for 1–2 minutes. Spread pudding over the top of
the first layer in the baking pan and refrigerate.

 5. In a metal bowl over a pot of simmering water,
melt the chocolate and butter, stirring occasionally. Let it cool for 5 minutes, then pour it over the
second layer.

 6. Refrigerate for 30 minutes, then cut into 1 by 2
inch bars and serve.

Yield: About 2 dozen bars

Storage: Cover Nanaimo bars with plastic wrap and refrigerate them for up to 2 weeks; freeze them for several
months.

 ## PECAN PIE BARS

General
Description: *No proper Southern picnic is complete without pecan pie
on the table, and with these delectable bars you can
bring that same classic flavor to any occasion.* Despite
pecan pie's deep entrenchment in U.S. Southern cuisine, pecan pie bars are a fairly recent addition to
this rich culinary tradition. Corn syrup is one of the
primary ingredients, and the process of refining corn
syrup wasn't perfected until the 1880s. The first

published pecan pie recipe dates to 1925. Interestingly, the popular corn syrup brand, Karo, claims that the wife of a Karo executive "discovered" the "Karo Pie" in the 1930s. It is more likely that the pecan pie was developed by French-Cajun chefs in New Orleans, often using Karo brand corn syrup. In either case, pecan pie recipes have become sources of pride for countless families, and these bars are surely no exception.

Serving
Suggestions:
❀ ❄ ▱

Pecan pies are standard fare during Thanksgiving and Christmas throughout the Southern United States. These easily transported bars allow you to bring this delightful dish to any occasion.

Baking Notes:

These bars are easy as pie. Light corn syrup is just as sweet as dark corn syrup, but it has a lighter flavor; use whichever you prefer.

Recipe:

Crust:
2 cups all-purpose flour
¹/₂ cup sugar
¹/₄ teaspoon salt
1 cup cold unsalted butter, cut into pieces

Filling:
4 eggs
1¹/₂ cups corn syrup
1¹/₂ cups light brown sugar

3 tablespoons unsalted butter, melted
1 teaspoon vanilla extract
2 cups pecan halves

 1.   Preheat oven to 350°F. Line a 9 by 13 inch pan with
aluminum foil, leaving enough to hang over the edge
and act as handles to remove bars after baking.
Grease foil with cooking spray.

2.   In a stand mixer, mix the crust ingredients on low
speed until a coarse meal is formed. (This process can
also be done in a food processor.)

3.   Pour the dough into the prepared pan and gently press
into the bottom, making sure it is level.

4.   Bake for 20 minutes until it is golden, firm, and dry
to the touch. While the crust is baking, prepare the
filling.

5.   Using a stand mixer, beat together eggs, corn syrup,
sugar, butter, and vanilla at medium speed until evenly mixed. Stir in pecans, decrease speed to low, and
mix until just combined.

6.   As soon as crust is done, pour filling directly into the
pan and return it to the oven; bake for 25 minutes or
until firm. Cool completely on a wire rack before
cutting.

7. **Using a sharp chef's knife, cut the long side into five strips, then cut four across the short side to create 20 squares.**

Yield: About 2 dozen

Storage: Store in an airtight container for up to 1 week.

Variation: ***Chocolate Pecan Pie Bars***
Make the crust per original recipe. When making the filling, combine the corn syrup with 6 oz of semisweet chocolate in a small saucepan. Heat on stove over low heat until the chocolate is melted. Remove from heat and stir in the rest of the filling ingredients; be sure the melted chocolate is not too hot or it will cook the eggs. Pour the filling over the baked crust and bake per original recipe.

50. RAINBOW COOKIES

General Description: *Rainbow cookies are elegant, eyecatching cookies made of three stacked layers of almond paste dough covered in chocolate. The almond paste is tinted different colors, which are typically pink, yellow, and green.* Rainbow cookies are also known as *Italian tri-color cookies*, *Venetian cookies*, and sometimes *7-layer cookies* (not to be confused with American 7-layer bars or **magic**

cookie bars). They are also sometimes called Neopol-
itan cookies, but this is a misnomer. (Neapolitan
cookies are typically flat butter-style cookies made
from three different colored doughs.)

The complexity of this cookie almost makes it
more like a miniature layer cake than a cookie. Some
versions of the rainbow cookie use only almond
extract, but the most authentic versions are made
with almond paste. Rainbow cookies are mostly
found in America; they are most popular in New
York City and are a common sight in many of the
city's bakeries.

History:	Rainbow cookies are associated with Christmas; kosher versions are made for Passover.
Serving Suggestions:	Because the dough can be tinted different colors, you can create different themes for different holidays.
Baking Notes:	Use a good quality almond paste for this recipe. Almond paste is similar to marzipan but generally has a higher percentage of almonds and therefore a stronger almond flavor. It is best used in baking.
Recipe:	**4 eggs, separated** **10 oz almond paste** **1¼ cups softened unsalted butter** **1 cup sugar**

1 teaspoon vanilla extract
¹/₂ teaspoon almond extract
2 cups all-purpose flour
¹/₂ teaspoon salt
6 drops green food coloring
6 drops red food coloring
6 tablespoons seedless raspberry preserves
1¹/₂ cups (10 oz) bittersweet chocolate, chopped

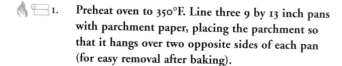

1. Preheat oven to 350°F. Line three 9 by 13 inch pans with parchment paper, placing the parchment so that it hangs over two opposite sides of each pan (for easy removal after baking).

2. In a stand mixer with the whisk attachment, whip egg whites on high speed until stiff peaks form. Transfer whites to a large metal bowl and set aside.

3. Chop almond paste into small chunks, about ¹/₄ inch.

4. In a stand mixer, beat butter on medium speed for several minutes until smooth. Add almond paste, and beat on medium speed until light in color and fully incorporated.

5. Add sugar, and beat to combine. Add egg yolks and vanilla and almond extracts, and mix to combine.

6. Combine flour and salt, and add it to the dough

in 3 additions, mixing thoroughly between each.

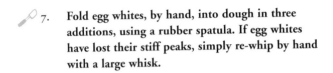

7. Fold egg whites, by hand, into dough in three additions, using a rubber spatula. If egg whites have lost their stiff peaks, simply re-whip by hand with a large whisk.

8. Divide dough into 3 equal portions and place in 3 mixing bowls. Add green food coloring to one bowl and red to another and mix each to combine. Leave the third bowl untinted.

9. Spread each bowl of dough into individual pans, using an offset spatula to even out the surface of the dough.

10. Bake for 8 to 11 minutes, rotating the pan halfway through, until top and edges begin to turn golden. Let cool for a few minutes, then carefully lift (or turn out if necessary) each sheet onto a wire rack to finish cooling.

11. Once cool, flip each cookie layer onto a flat surface and peel off parchment paper. Flip green cookie layer onto a large piece of plastic wrap.

12. Spread a thin layer of raspberry preserves on top of the green cookie layer. Place the plain (untinted) layer of cookie on top and line up the edges.

13. Spread a thin layer of raspberry preserves on top of the plain cookie layer, then place the red cookie layer on top.

14. Wrap up cookie layers with plastic wrap. Sandwich cookie between two heavy cutting boards or two large books, and refrigerate. Chill for at least 3 hours, flipping cookie several times.

15. Remove cookie from refrigerator and place on cutting board. Using a serrated knife, cut six $1^{1}/_{2}$-inch horizontal strips lengthwise (13 inches long).

16. Set up a wire rack with a cookie sheet underneath to catch any chocolate drips. Place 2 cookie strips on the rack, leaving enough room between to reach all sides with a spatula.

17. Melt chocolate in a metal bowl set over a simmering pot of water on the stove, stirring occasionally so it melts evenly.

18. Pour chocolate along tops of cookies, allowing it to drip over the sides. Spread chocolate evenly, using an offset spatula, to cover top and sides.

19. Transfer to a flat surface and allow chocolate to set (the chocolate is not tempered, so it will not set completely and will remain slightly tacky). Repeat

process with remaining cookie strips, reheating chocolate as needed.

20. Once chocolate is set, cut strips into individual pieces, approximately 3/4-inch in length. Clean knife in between cuts for a flawless cookie.

Yield: About 7 dozen 1 1/2 by 3/4 inch cookies

Storage: Store in an airtight container for up to 3 weeks, and they actually improve with age. Chocolate-coated cookie strips may be frozen before cutting for several months.

51. **ROSEMARY PARMESAN BISCOTTI**

General Description: *Laced with aromatic leaves of rosemary and parmesan cheese, rosemary parmesan biscotti are a savory variation on the traditionally sweeter **biscotti**.* These biscotti complement a range of dishes.

History: Biscotti have been around since Roman times, when legionnaires took these travel-worthy baked goods on the road. Biscotti became a classic in the Tuscany region of Italy, where original recipes use almonds as their base. Savory biscotti recipes are gaining in popularity, from pesto biscotti to two-cheese varieties.

Serving Suggestions:	Serve savory biscotti with wine or cocktails before dinner. They are also perfect for breakfast, served as bruschetta or with prosciutto, fresh scrambled eggs, and spinach.

Baking Notes:	See **Biscotti** on pages 131–35 for tips on shaping and slicing the logs of dough.

Recipe:

1 3/4 cups all-purpose flour
1/2 teaspoon salt
1/4 teaspoon ground pepper
1 teaspoon baking powder
2 sprigs fresh rosemary, chopped (or 2 teaspoons dried rosemary)
3 1/2 tablespoons freshly grated parmesan cheese
2 eggs
3 tablespoons unsalted butter, melted

 1. Preheat oven to 350°F. Grease a cookie sheet or line with parchment paper.

 2. In a stand mixer, combine flour, salt, pepper, baking powder, rosemary, and parmesan cheese. Add eggs, one at a time, and mix after each addition to fully incorporate. Add butter and mix to combine.

3. Turn out dough onto a lightly floured surface. Use hands to form dough into one mass, then divide it into two equal pieces.

4. Roll each piece of dough into a log approximately 1 1/2 inches in diameter. Transfer each to cookie sheets, spacing them about 4–5 inches apart. Use palm of hand to flatten each log until they are 2–2 1/2 inches across.

5. Bake for 25–28 minutes, rotating sheet halfway through. Remove from oven, and let biscotti logs rest on the cookie sheet for 20 minutes. Logs will still be slightly spongy to the touch, similar to a dense bread.

6. Lower the oven temperature to 250°F.

7. After 20 minutes, remove biscotti logs from pan and place on cutting board. Using a serrated knife, in one quick motion for each slice, cut log into 1/2-inch slices. Return the slices, cut side up, to the cookie sheet. Place the slices right next to each other, filling up the entire sheet, as the biscotti will no longer expand.

8. Bake biscotti for 30 minutes. Remove and cool on wire racks. Slices will be slightly soft while warm but will harden when cooled.

Yield: About 2 dozen biscotti

Storage: These cookies can be sealed airtight between layers of wax or parchment paper for up to 1 month. They can be frozen for up to 4 months.

52. **TURTLE BARS**

General
Description:

Turtle bars don't resemble turtles, but they are just as sweet and addictive as the turtle candy inspired by the shelled reptile. Turtle bars are an American cookie composed of a buttery shortbread base topped with pecans, over which a rich caramel is poured. The bars are topped with chocolate chips or a layer of chocolate glaze. The bars are rich, sticky, and gooey, and usually served cut in squares, similar to **brownies** or **blondies**.

History:

Turtle bars were named after turtle candy, a classic American confection made of caramel and chocolate poured over four or five pecan halves that are arranged to look like the head and feet of a turtle. Over time, the flavor combination of pecans, caramel, and chocolate has become associated with the term *turtle*, as seen in turtle ice cream sundaes or turtle cheesecake.

Serving
Suggestions:

Turtle bars are already rich and sweet. But if you would like a more intensely sweet flavor, sprinkle them with peanut butter chips or mini marshmallows.

Baking Notes:

Before you add the topping, be sure the cookie crust is fully baked so it doesn't become soggy. Coarsely chopped pecans are the best size for the bars, as whole pecans make the bars difficult to slice. Wipe the knife clean between cuts to create neat bars.

Recipe: **Base:**
1 1/2 cups all-purpose flour
1/2 cup dark brown sugar
1/4 teaspoon salt
1/2 cup cold unsalted butter

Topping:
1/3 cup heavy cream
3/4 cup unsalted butter
1/4 teaspoon salt
3/4 cup light brown sugar
1 1/2 cups pecans
1 cup chocolate chips

1. Preheat oven to 350°F. Line a 9 by 13 inch pan with aluminum foil, leaving enough to hang over the edge and act as handles to remove bars after baking. Grease foil with cooking spray.

2. Combine flour, sugar, and salt in a food processor and blend briefly to combine.

3. Cut butter in small pieces and sprinkle over flour mixture. Process until the mixture resembles coarse crumbs.

4. Press the mixture evenly into the bottom of the pan. Bake for 18 to 20 minutes, until the crust is golden and firm and dry. Leave the oven on at the

same temperature.

 5. Combine the cream, butter, salt, and brown sugar in a saucepan and bring to a boil for about 1 minute.

6. Spread the pecans over the top of the crust. Pour the hot caramel filling evenly over the pecans.

7. Bake for 15–20 minutes, until the caramel topping darkens.

8. Remove from oven and sprinkle the chocolate chips over the hot topping. Let sit for a few moments and then use a knife or offset spatula to spread the melted chocolate evenly over the top.

9. Chill the bars in the refrigerator for about 30 minutes or until the bars have fully set before slicing them.

10. Using foil as handles, pull bars from pan and place on cutting board. Cut long side into 9 strips, then cut 4 strips across the short side, creating 36 bars. Wipe the knife clean between cuts.

Yield: 3 dozen bars

Storage: Store in an airtight container for up to 1 week.

Molded Cookies

53. **FINANCIERS**

General
Description:

Financiers are miniature French teacakes made with ground almonds and browned butter. The almonds give the financiers a sweet nuttiness, while the browned butter, or *beurre noisette*, enhances the caramel and nut flavors. Financiers are usually made in small rectangular molds, but they can be found in a variety of forms, from rounds to boat-shaped *barquettes*. Sometimes they are referred to as *brown butter cakes*. In Australia, a version of financier is called a *friand*.

History:

Financiers were created in Paris in the late 1800s. The name for these little teacakes comes from their association with the financial district. The story is that they were invented by a pastry chef named Lasne, who wanted to create a quick snack that busy bankers could eat easily without getting crumbs or fillings on their suits. The financiers' classic, rectangular shape is said to resemble the bars of gold that banks used in the 1800s.

Serving
Suggestions:

Financiers are versatile and adaptable. They can be shaped like anything from miniature muffins to hearts. Financier batter adapts well to additional flavors, including cocoa powder, espresso, spices, and herbs. A simple but lovely variation is to drop fresh berries into the batter right before baking. Financier batter also keeps well in the refrigerator for a couple of days, so this is an excellent make-ahead cookie. Financiers are wonderful on their own with a cup of tea, or as a base for desserts; they go well with ice cream or fresh fruit.

Baking Notes:

Be sure to let the browned butter cool before using it, without letting it resolidify. If you use the butter while it is too hot, it will ruin the batter. When you are ready to bake the financiers, be sure to grease the pans well or the financiers will stick.

Recipe:

¹/₂ **cup unsalted butter**
1¹/₄ **cups confectioners' sugar**
¹/₃ **cup all-purpose flour**
¹/₄ **teaspoon salt**
¹/₂ **cup ground almonds**
4 **egg whites**

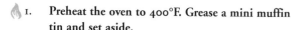

1. **Preheat the oven to 400°F. Grease a mini muffin tin and set aside.**

2. **Place the butter in a skillet and melt over medium heat. Let the butter keep cooking until the solids separate and turn golden brown. Swirling the butter, continue heating until the liquid changes from a light yellow to a deep golden—be careful not to take it too far or it will burn. Remove from heat**

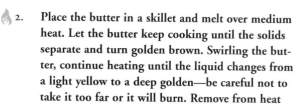

and strain butter into a bowl. Let the butter cool while you make the rest of the batter.

3. Sift confectioners' sugar, flour, and salt into a stand mixer bowl. Add ground almonds and mix together until combined.

4. Add in the egg whites and mix together until it becomes a smooth batter, about 3 minutes.

5. Be sure the browned butter is cooled, and add to the batter. Beat for a few minutes on medium speed until smooth and combined.

6. Divide batter among mini muffin tins, filling about 3/4 full. Bake for 12–14 minutes, rotating halfway through. The financiers should turn brown and develop a crisp crust.

7. Remove from oven and let cool on wire racks for about 5 minutes. Unmold the financiers and let them finish cooling on the racks.

Yield: About 2 dozen financiers

Storage: Store in an airtight container for about 1 week. You can warm financiers in an oven for a few minutes before serving.

54. **FORTUNE COOKIES**

General
Description:

The distinctive fortune cookie is a crisp cookie that is made from a flat disc of dough folded up and around a small strip of paper. Words of wisdom, mock predictions, and lucky numbers are written on these strips, giving the fortune cookie its name. The cookie is golden and crispy, similar to a **tuile** but thicker, and usually vanilla flavored. Fortune cookies are served almost exclusively in Chinese restaurants in America and Canada as a dessert; the cookie was not invented in China and it is actually absent from restaurants there.

History:

There are a few competing theories about the origin of the fortune cookie, but it is accepted that the cookie was invented in California and not in China. A Chinese immigrant living in Los Angeles, David Jung, claims to have created the fortune cookie in 1918. He made the cookies at his shop, placed inspirational messages inside them, and gave them away to the poor he saw around his shop. A second theory holds that the cookie was created by a Japanese immigrant in San Francisco. Makoto Hagiwara supposedly made his cookies as a version of *senebi*, a crispy Japanese rice cookie, in 1914. Hagiwara gave the cookies with notes tucked inside to his friends, and later started serving them at the Japanese Tea Garden in Golden Gate Park.

Serving
Suggestions:

Because of their simple, unadorned taste, fortune
cookies are a nice, light ending to a meal. They are
particularly good served with fresh fruit. The ability
to put custom messages inside handmade fortune
cookies also makes them wonderful party favors. The
vanilla flavor of the cookie can be easily adapted by
adding a few drops of almond, orange, or lemon
extract, or perhaps adding some cocoa powder to
make a chocolate version of the cookie.

Baking Notes:

As with tuiles, the easiest way to get a perfect circle
of batter is to make a template. You can quickly
make one by cutting a circle out of a plastic can lid.
It takes a fast hand and practice to shape the hot circles of dough into the fortune cookie form; wear
cotton gloves to protect your fingers.

Recipe:

2 egg whites
¹/₂ cup sugar
¹/₈ teaspoon salt
²/₃ cup all-purpose flour
¹/₃ cup unsalted butter, melted and cooled
1 tablespoon water

 1.

**In a stand mixer with the paddle attachment, beat
egg whites on medium speed until just frothy.**

2.

**Add sugar and mix to combine. Add in salt and
flour and mix to combine. Add in the butter and**

water and mix until the batter is a smooth paste.

3. Cover dough and chill in the refrigerator for about 30 minutes.

4. During this time, write fortunes on strips of paper—the papers should be about 2 $^{1}/_{2}$ inches long and $^{1}/_{4}$ inch wide to fit inside the cookie.

5. Preheat the oven to 350°F. Line several cookie sheets with silicone baking mats.

6. Using a stencil, spread tablespoons of batter onto the cookie sheets with an offset spatula, spacing them about 2 inches apart. Be sure to spread the batter as thinly and evenly as possible—if it is too thick it will not bake properly. Do not place more than 4 cookies per sheet, as they will harden very quickly out of the oven and you will not have time to shape them.

7. Bake for 6–8 minutes, until the tops look golden and feel dry. Do not let them get too dark or they will be too firm to shape.

8. Place cookie sheets on wire rack. Immediately place a fortune in the center of one cookie. Fold the cookie in half to form a semicircle. Holding the folded end up, push the center of the fold in

while pulling the two outside corners down to form the traditional fortune cookie shape.

9. **Let fortune cookies finish cooling on the rack while you repeat with the rest of the cookies. If the cookies get too hard while you are forming them, place them in the oven for about 30 seconds to soften.**

Yield: About 1 dozen cookies

Storage: Store in an airtight container for about 1 week.

55. **GINGERSNAPS**

General Description: *Gingersnaps are dark brown, flat, crisp cookies with a wonderfully strong gingery, spicy flavor.* Sometimes they have a round shape with a crinkly top similar to **molasses spice cookies**, but they can also have flat, smooth surfaces and sharp edges. Gingersnaps can be made with molasses, but they should be thin and crispy, and usually have a more intense, peppery flavor than molasses spice cookies. In Europe, they are known as *pepperkakor*, which are typically made with the dough rolled very thin and various shapes cut out. They are one of the most popular Christmas cookies in Scandinavia.

History: See also the entries on **gingerbread**, **lebkuchen**, and
molasses spice cookies. Gingersnaps are just one of
the many cakes and cookies that were invented with
the introduction of ginger to medieval Europe in the
11th century. They became traditional to make
many of these cookies for Christmas and other winter festivals. The name *gingersnaps* likely comes from
the "snap" made when biting into one of the cookies.

Serving   With their bold spiciness, gingersnaps are a pleasant
Suggestions: alternative to other, sweeter cookies. They are best
enjoyed with a glass of milk or cup of coffee. If you
would like increase the intensity of the flavor, tinker
with quantities and varieties of spices used. Adding 2
teaspoons black or white pepper is one way to turn up
the heat. You can also add bits of chopped, crystal-
lized ginger to the dough to add some chewy interest.

Baking Notes: Since the taste and quality of these cookies are
dependent on the quality of the spices used, be sure
to check your ingredients for freshness. Old spices
might make your cookies taste stale, or worse, add
little to the flavor. To best preserve the crisp snappi-
ness of these cookies, store them in an airtight container between sheets of wax paper as soon as they
have completely cooled.

Recipe: **3 cups all-purpose flour**
2¹/₂ teaspoons baking soda

$^1/_4$ teaspoon salt
1 cup softened unsalted butter
$^3/_4$ cup sugar
$^1/_4$ cup light brown sugar
$1^1/_2$ teaspoons ground ginger
1 teaspoon ground cinnamon
$^1/_4$ teaspoon white pepper
1 egg
$^1/_3$ cup molasses
Extra sugar for rolling

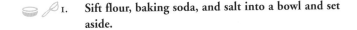

1. Sift flour, baking soda, and salt into a bowl and set aside.

2. In a stand mixer, cream butter and sugars on medium speed for several minutes until smooth, light, and fluffy. Add spices and mix until combined.

3. Add egg and mix to combine. Add molasses and mix to combine.

4. Add flour mixture and mix to just combine.

5. Turn dough out onto lightly floured surface. Roll dough into a 12-inch log and wrap in parchment or plastic wrap. Refrigerate at least 30 minutes or until firm enough to slice. Dough may be refrigerated up to 2 days or stored in the freezer, wrapped

airtight, for 2 weeks (thaw in refrigerator overnight before using).

 6. Preheat oven to 350°F. Grease several cookie sheets. Fill a small bowl with the sugar reserved for rolling.

7. Using a sharp chef's knife, cut slices ¹/4 to ³/8 inch thick. Coat slices in sugar and place on sheets about 2 inches apart.

 8. Bake for 6–10 minutes; for chewy cookies, remove from oven when each cookie is just holding its shape when nudged. For crispy cookies, bake until edges are set and center is slightly soft. Cool sheets on wire racks for a couple minutes before transferring cookies directly onto wire racks with a spatula to finish cooling.

Yield: About 5¹/2 dozen cookies

Storage: Store in an airtight container for up to 4 days.

56. **GREEK BUTTER COOKIES (KOURABIETHES)**

General Description: *Veiled in a thick snowfall of powdered sugar, these buttery almond shortbread crescents from Greece make for a striking celebratory cookie.* These cookies (known as *kourabiethes* in Greek) are primarily baked at Christmastime, and a snow-white pile of butter cookies is often the crowning touch on a Greek table at dinner.

History:

These cookies have long been a central part of Greek Christmas celebrations. They are also popular throughout the year for celebrations such as baptisms, weddings and New Year's Eve. In Crete, they are traditionally served the morning of Easter.

Serving Suggestions:

Serve Greek butter cookies warm with a cup of coffee or a scoop of vanilla ice cream. For New Year's, serve them with **Greek Honey Macaroons** and champagne.

Baking Notes:

These cookies are usually spiced with a bit of ground cloves, but you can omit them for a less spicy flavor. Greek brandy is traditionally used in these cookies, but any brandy will do. Alternatively, you can use ouzo, the classic Greek anise-flavored liqueur.

Recipe:

1 cup softened unsalted butter
1/4 cup confectioners' sugar
1 egg yolk
1/2 teaspoon vanilla extract
1/4 teaspoon almond extract
1 tablespoon Greek brandy or ouzo
1/2 cup ground blanched almonds

¹/8 teaspoon ground cloves (optional)

2¹/2 cups all-purpose flour

Confectioners' sugar for dusting

 1. Preheat the oven to 300°F. Line several cookie sheets with parchment paper or silicone baking mats.

 2. In a stand mixer, cream butter and confectioners' sugar on medium speed for several minutes until light and fluffy. Add the egg, both extracts, and brandy and mix until combined.

 3. Add ground almonds and cloves, and mix on low speed until just combined. Add the flour gradually and mix until fully combined.

 4. You can shape the dough into three traditional shapes. For domes: roll tablespoons of dough into balls. For crescents: roll tablespoons of dough into balls and form into a crescent shape. For tapered ovals: roll tablespoons of dough into balls and then pinch the ends to form a "football" shape. Place cookies on sheets about 1 inch apart.

 5. Bake for 16 to 20 minutes, rotating sheets halfway through, until the bottoms are just lightly colored. Remove sheets from oven and place on wire racks. Immediately sift confectioner's sugar over the cookies, making sure they are thoroughly covered. Let cookies

finish cooling on sheets.

Yield: About 3 dozen cookies

Storage: Store in an airtight container for up to 2 weeks.

57. **GREEK EASTER COOKIES (KOULOURAKIA)**

General Description:

Glazed a pale gold and sprinkled with sesame seeds, these ring-shaped desserts come from Greece. Koulourakia (pronounced coo-loo-RAK-ia) means "little ringed loaf" or "little belt," but these cookies can be found in a variety of other shapes, such as twists, braids, and S curves. While readily available throughout the year, and commonly served with coffee, they are particularly associated with Easter.

History:

Easter is one of most important Greek holidays, and *koulourakia* are made as part of the Easter Sunday feast. These cookies are traditionally made on Holy Thursday as part of the many rituals of the week leading up to Easter. Their S-shaped form is meant to resemble a snake, and may have been started on the island of Crete, where the ancient Minoans believed snakes to have special healing powers.

Serving
Suggestions:

These cookies are excellent dunked into a cup of strong dark coffee at breakfast or with a cup of tea as a pre-bedtime treat.

Baking Notes:

You can form these cookies in a multitude of creative shapes besides the traditional rings and snakes. Remember to keep all the cookies about the same size so they bake evenly.

Recipe:

2²/₃ cups all-purpose flour
2 teaspoons baking powder
¹/₈ teaspoon salt
²/₃ cup softened unsalted butter
²/₃ cup sugar
2 eggs
1¹/₂ teaspoons orange zest
1 egg yolk, for egg wash
1¹/₂ teaspoons milk, for egg wash
2 tablespoons sesame seeds

1. **Preheat the oven to 350°F. Line several cookie sheets with parchment paper or silicone baking mats.**

2. **Sift the flour, baking powder, and salt into a bowl and set aside.**

3. **In a stand mixer, cream butter and sugar on medium speed for several minutes until light and fluffy. Add the egg and orange zest and mix until combined.**

4. Add the flour mixture, and mix on low speed just until combined.

 5. Roll tablespoon-sized balls of dough into 4-inch-long ropes. Form the ropes into rings or S shapes. You can also make a twisted belt shape by placing one rope of dough on top of another and twisting them into a loop. Place cookies on sheets about 2 inches apart.

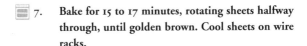 6. Whisk egg yolk and milk together to make an egg wash. Brush the tops of the cookies with the egg wash and sprinkle with sesame seeds.

 7. Bake for 15 to 17 minutes, rotating sheets halfway through, until golden brown. Cool sheets on wire racks.

Yield: About 3 dozen cookies

Storage: Store in an airtight container for up to 2 weeks.

---

58. 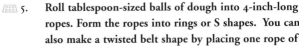 **GREEK HONEY MACAROONS (MELOMAKARONA)**

General Description: *Greek* melomakarona *are distinctive and indulgent oval-shaped cookies soaked in a spiced honey syrup and sprinkled with walnuts.* Also known as *phoenikia*, these delicious cookies are ubiquitous throughout Greece during the Christmas holidays. Their name (pronounced *meh-lo-mah-KAH-ro-nah*) literally means "honey macaroon," though these honey-soaked cookies are quite distinct from **coconut macaroons** and **French macarons**.

History: Greek honey macaroons are Christmas and New Year's Day traditions. Macaroons have appeared in cookbooks since the late 1600s, and they have been served with wine or liqueurs as after-dinner refreshment ever since.

Serving Suggestions: Give the gift of these traditional Greek cookies at Christmas, or serve them as midnight treats to ring in the New Year.

Baking Notes: Don't overwork or flatten the dough; it must be airy and thick enough to soak up the honey syrup. Local honey—ranging from citrus flower honey to Greek thyme honey—gives cookies a unique light flavor and scent.

Recipe:
¹/₄ teaspoon baking soda
2 teaspoons lemon juice
3 cups all-purpose flour
¹/₂ cup sugar
¹/₂ teaspoon baking powder
¹/₈ teaspoon salt

3/4 cup olive oil (not extra virgin)

1/4 cup lukewarm water

1 tablespoon brandy

1 teaspoon lemon zest

3/8 teaspoon ground cinnamon

3/8 teaspoon ground cloves

Topping:

1/3 cup sesame seeds, toasted

1/2 cup walnut pieces, toasted and finely chopped

1/4 teaspoon ground cinnamon

Honey syrup:

1/2 cup water

1/2 cup sugar

1/4 cup honey

2 teaspoons lemon juice

1/2 cinnamon stick

3 whole cloves

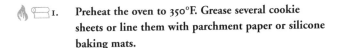 1. Preheat the oven to 350°F. Grease several cookie sheets or line them with parchment paper or silicone baking mats.

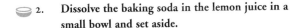 2. Dissolve the baking soda in the lemon juice in a small bowl and set aside.

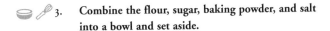 3. Combine the flour, sugar, baking powder, and salt into a bowl and set aside.

4. In a stand mixer, combine the baking soda mixture with the olive oil, water, brandy, lemon zest, cinnamon, and nutmeg. Mix on medium speed for 2 minutes.

5. With the mixer running on low speed, add the flour mixture slowly. Mix until the dough is combined and no longer sticky.

6. Roll tablespoon-sized balls of dough into cylinders 2 inches long and 1 inch wide. Form the cylinders into ovals and place on sheets about 2 inches apart.

7. Bake for 28–30 minutes, rotating sheets halfway through, until firm and golden brown. Cool sheets on wire racks.

8. While the cookies are cooling, make the topping by combining all the topping ingredients in a small bowl.

9. When the cookies are cool, make the syrup. In a medium saucepan, combine all the syrup ingredients and bring to a boil over medium heat, stirring occasionally.

10. Reduce heat to low and boil for 5 minutes. Remove from heat and skim off any foam from the surface. Remove the cinnamon stick and cloves.

11. **Line a cookie sheet with foil or parchment paper. Place 6–8 cookies at a time in the syrup (use caution as the syrup will be hot) for 30 seconds. Remove cookies with a slotted spoon, shake off excess syrup, and place them on the sheets. Sprinkle immediately with topping. Wait 2 hours before storing.**

Yield: About 3 dozen cookies

Storage: Store in an airtight container for up to 7 days.

59. INDONESIAN PINEAPPLE COOKIES (KUE NASTAR)

General Description: *These beautiful golden, pineapple-filled cookies are a classic Indonesian dessert.* They are also known as *kue nastar* (Indonesian) or *ananas taart* (Dutch).

History: These cookies have long been popular in the city of Depok, but have recently become a fixture across Indonesia, frequenting the menus of fancy restaurants and village banquets alike. They are usually served during the Christmas holidays or the Islamic holiday of *Eid ul-Fitr*, which celebrates the end of Ramadan. Indonesia has a long tradition of delicious cakes and pastries.

Serving
Suggestions:

Muslim Indonesians serve these cookies as part of the great feasts that are traditional on *Eid ul-Fitr*. But Indonesian pineapple cookies are perfect served at any religious or secular celebration, and they add a little tropical kick to the winter holidays.

Baking Notes:

These cookies are also formed by squeezing dough out a *nastar* mold; if you can find one, they make beautifully shaped cookies. The dough is meant to be soft, which gives the baked cookies a very tender texture. If you have trouble filling the balls of dough because they are too soft, try making smaller balls, filling the indentations with jam, and then sandwiching two of them together and sealing the edges.

Recipe:

1 3/4 cups all-purpose flour
1/4 teaspoon salt
1 cup softened unsalted butter
1/4 cup confectioners' sugar
3 egg yolks
1/2 teaspoon vanilla extract
1 cup pineapple jam or preserves
1 egg, beaten, for egg wash

1. Sift flour and salt into a bowl and set aside.

2. Using a stand mixer, cream butter and confectioners' sugar on medium speed for several minutes until light and fluffy. Add the egg yolks, one at a time. Add

the vanilla and mix until combined.

3. Add the flour mixture and mix until fully incorporated.

4. Cover dough and refrigerate for about 30 minutes until firm.

5. Preheat oven to 325°F. Line several cookie sheets with parchment paper or silicone baking mats.

6. Roll the dough into 1-inch balls and place on cookie sheets. Make a depression in the center of each dough ball, and fill with about $1/2$ teaspoon of the pineapple filling. Pinch the edges of the dough back around the filling, and turn seam side down. Place on sheets about 2 inches apart.

7. Brush the tops of each cookie with egg wash. Bake 15–18 minutes, rotating sheets halfway through, until shiny and golden. Cool on wire racks.

Yield: About 2 dozen cookies

Storage: Store in an airtight container for up to 1 week.

60. **ITALIAN EASTER COOKIES (TARALLI DOLCI)**

General Description:

Draped in a glaze of icing and a confetti of sprinkles, these ring-shaped snacks could be mistaken for donuts. With their crisp texture and light citrus aroma, these sweet Italian cookies, known as *taralli dolci* or *taralli dolci di Pasqua*, are traditionally made for Easter.

History:

Throughout the year, regular *taralli* are boiled like pretzels throughout Italy, where they have been popular street fare for centuries. As early as the 8th century, they were made by mixing lard and spices with scraps of bread dough, and sold from carts on city streets.

Serving Suggestions:

These cookies are ideal for a traditional Italian Easter Sunday dinner. They are also delicious with a cup of coffee as an after-dinner treat or in the summertime with a cold glass of milk or lemonade.

Baking Notes:

These cookies will puff up quite a bit in the oven. They can be served without the glaze.

Recipe:

1 3/4 cups plus 2 tablespoons all-purpose flour
1 1/2 teaspoons baking powder
pinch of salt
2 eggs
1/3 cup sugar

4 tablespoons unsalted butter, melted
1¹/₂ teaspoons vanilla extract

Glaze:
1 teaspoon light corn syrup
4 teaspoons water
¹/₄ teaspoon vanilla extract
1 cup confectioners' sugar, sifted
Colored sprinkles or nonpareils for decorating

1. Preheat the oven to 350°F. Grease several cookie sheets or line with parchment paper.

2. Sift the flour, baking powder, and salt into a bowl and set aside.

3. In a stand mixer, beat eggs on medium speed for a minute.

4. Add sugar gradually, and mix on medium speed until combined. Reduce mixer speed to low and add butter and vanilla.

5. Add the flour mixture, and mix on low speed just until combined.

6. Roll tablespoon-sized balls of dough into 6-inch long ropes. Form the ropes into rings. Place cookies on sheets about 2 inches apart.

⏳ 7. **Let cookies sit for 15 minutes before baking.**

🍳 🔪 8. **Bake for 15 to 17 minutes, rotating sheets halfway through, until golden brown. Cool cookie sheets on wire racks for 5 minutes before transferring cookies directly onto wire racks with a metal spatula to finish cooling.**

🔥 🥄 9. **For the glaze: Combine corn syrup, water, and vanilla extract in a small saucepan and heat over medium heat until warm. Remove from heat and stir in confectioners' sugar, stirring until combined.**

🎆 10. **Dip tops of cookies in the glaze, shake off excess, and place on wire rack. Immediately sprinkle with colored sprinkles or nonpareils. Let glaze set before serving.**

Yield: About 2 dozen cookies

Storage: Store in an airtight container for up to 2 weeks.

🍱

61a–b. 📷 **JAM THUMBPRINTS**

General Description: *These little shortbread treats are bejeweled by a dollop of sweet fruit jam in their centers.* Thumbprints aren't defined by a particular cookie dough recipe but by the characteristic thumbprint indentations in their centers. Jam thumbprints are among the most popular. These are often prepared with a variety of jams in each batch to create a colorful array.

History:	Thumbprint cookie dough is usually a variation of an English or Scottish shortbread. Jam became popular for its longevity and sweetness in the 1500s, when sugar became affordable through sugar plantations.

Serving
Suggestions:

Thumbprints are classic Christmas cookies, birthday cookies, and gifts. Prettily colored buttercream thumbprints (page 201) are easy-to-bake, festive cookies and a great way to bring the kids into the kitchen.

Baking Notes:

Thumbprints are so simple that it's easy and fun to vary the recipe. Fill thumbprints with ganache, Nutella, or lemon curd.

Recipe:

1 cup all-purpose flour
1/4 teaspoon salt
1/2 cup softened unsalted butter
1/3 cup sugar
1 egg yolk
1/2 teaspoon vanilla extract
1/2 teaspoon almond extract
1/2 cup assorted fruit jams

 1. **Preheat oven to 350°F. Line several cookie sheets with parchment paper.**

2. In a small bowl, whisk together flour and salt.

3. In a stand mixer, cream butter and sugar at medium speed for several minutes until light and fluffy. Add egg yolk, vanilla, and almond extract, and mix until combined.

4. Reduce speed to low and gradually incorporate the flour and salt, mixing only until just incorporated.

5. Roll the dough into 3/4-inch balls. Press your thumb into the center of each, making a depression large enough to fit 1 teaspoon of filling. Place the cookies on cookie sheets and bake for 10 minutes.

6. Remove cookies from oven. Drop rounded teaspoonfuls of jam into the center of each cookie, then return cookies to the oven for 4–5 minutes, or until the edges begin to turn golden brown. Cool sheets on wire racks for 2 minutes before using a metal spatula to move cookies to wire racks to finish cooling.

Yield: About 2 dozen cookies

Storage: These cookies will keep for up to 3 weeks refrigerated in an airtight container, or frozen for up to 2 months.

Variations: **Buttercream Thumbprints**
Add the dollops of buttercream to the thumbprints once the cookies are done baking and have cooled. Tint buttercream with food coloring or flavor it with 1 teaspoon amaretto, espresso, or citrus extract.

Buttercream:
1 cup softened unsalted butter
3 cups confectioners' sugar
1 teaspoon vanilla extract
1¹/₂ tablespoons heavy cream

At low speed in a stand mixer, whisk together butter and sugar until light and creamy. Increase speed to medium and beat for 3 minutes. Add vanilla and cream, and beat until combined. Portion frosting into several separate dishes to tint it a variety of colors; add a few drops of food coloring to each, and stir to combine. Drop teaspoonfuls of frosting into thumbprints. Let frosting set for 30 minutes before serving.

62. **LADYFINGERS**

General
Description: *With their pale, delicate coloring and long, narrow form that resembles the gracefully tapering fingers of a refined lady, it is easy to see how ladyfingers got their name.* In Italy these soft, spongy cookies are called *savoiardi,* meaning "from Savoy." They are also called *sponge*

biscuits, *boudoir biscuits*, and *biscuits à la cuillier*. They are usually soft yellow and dusted with confectioners' sugar before baking to give them a crisp crust that yields to the light, sponge cake–like center.

Ladyfingers are a base for desserts such as tiramisu, charlottes, and trifles, where they are used to form an elegant border for the filling inside. Because they are often soaked in syrups or covered in soft mousses as part of a dessert, ladyfingers are sometimes made somewhat dry. Ladyfingers are part of the sponge cake or *genoise* cake family (cake made with no leaveners). Air is incorporated into the batter by vigorously whipping the eggs; these air bubbles are what give the cookies their light texture.

History:

Ladyfingers were first created in the Duchy of Savoy in the 15th century, to mark a visit from the king of France. Their popularity slowly spread through Europe, especially to Italy and England.

Serving Suggestions:

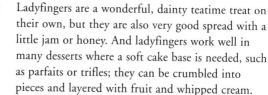

Ladyfingers are a wonderful, dainty teatime treat on their own, but they are also very good spread with a little jam or honey. And ladyfingers work well in many desserts where a soft cake base is needed, such as parfaits or trifles; they can be crumbled into pieces and layered with fruit and whipped cream. Ladyfingers are often the cake layer of choice for making tiramisu, as they soak up the espresso and rum flavors very well. Make beautiful charlottes by lining a trifle bowl with ladyfingers to form a border and filling the center with whipped cream, berries, or mousse.

Baking Notes:

Because ladyfingers depend on air whipped into the batter to provide leavening, it is important not to let the eggs deflate once they have been whipped. Fold egg whites into the dough using gentle, careful motions, and stop once it looks like they have just combined. Always use a lift-and-scoop motion, not a stirring motion, to avoid deflating the eggs. If you want slightly crisper, sturdier cookies, leave them in the oven for 5 more minutes, until they turn golden brown.

Recipe:

¹/₂ cup plus 2 tablespoons all-purpose flour
3 egg whites at room temperature
5 tablespoons plus ¹/₄ teaspoon sugar for whipping egg whites
3 egg yolks at room temperature
3 tablespoons plus 1 teaspoons sugar for whipping egg yolks
Confectioners' sugar for dusting

1. **Preheat oven to 375°F. Stack four cookie sheets together in pairs: You need to double up the sheets to avoid drying out the ladyfingers. Line the top sheets with parchment paper or a silicone baking mat. Fit a pastry bag with a #6 plain round pastry**

tip, and set aside.

 2. Sift the flour into a bowl and set aside.

 3. In a stand mixer with the whisk attachment, whip the whites on medium-high speed until foamy.

 4. With the mixer on low, add the sugar for the egg whites in a slow stream. Increase mixer speed to high and whip until stiff peaks form. Do not over-whip: Whites should be glossy, not chalky. Scrape whites into a separate bowl.

 5. In the stand mixer with the whisk attachment and a clean bowl, whip the egg yolks on medium-high speed for a few minutes to break up the yolks.

 6. Gradually add the sugar for the egg yolks in a slow stream. Whip on high speed until mixture is pale and thickened.

 7. Gently fold in the whipped whites in 3 additions using a spatula.

 8. Very gently fold in the sifted flour in 2 additions.

 9. Once you have finished the batter, work quickly before the batter deflates. Fill the pastry bag with half of the batter and pipe the batter onto the

cookie sheets. When piping, the tip of the pastry bag should be at a 45 degree angle to the pan. Gently pipe batter, forming ladyfingers that are ³/4 inch wide by 4 inches long.

 10. Continue piping the rest of the batter in the same manner. Once all the batter is piped, sift confectioners' sugar over the ladyfingers twice.

 11. Bake for 10 to 12 minutes or until lightly golden in color. Cool completely on the sheets before removing with a metal spatula.

Yield: About 3 dozen ladyfingers

Storage: Store in an airtight container for up to 3 days. If
 you are not going to use the ladyfingers right away, they will go stale quickly, so store them in the freezer until ready to use them.

63. **LEBKUCHEN**

General
Description: *Lebkuchen are traditional German Christmas cookies*
 made legendary by the folktale "Hansel and Gretel." Related to the many kinds of European **gingerbreads** and cookies, lebkuchen are made with honey instead of the molasses used in other recipes. They are usually formed by pressing the dough into a

carved wooden mold that imprints a design onto the top of the cookie. Gingerbread houses are often made out of large pieces of lebkuchen iced together.

History:

The German town of Nuremberg was a large producer of honey, and as a major trade city it had easy access to spices from the east, which may be why the city bakers developed lebkuchen, a unique version of the European gingerbread, in the 15th century. After *Grimms' Fairy Tales* were published in the 1800s, the story of Hansel and Gretel inspired Nuremberg bakers to make large edible houses of lebkuchen called *hexenhaeusle*, or witches' houses, thus beginning the tradition of gingerbread houses.

Serving Suggestions:

Lebkuchen are a classic holiday cookie and can be formed and decorated just like gingerbread. They can be simply drizzled with icing or piped with a fancy design. Because they are made with honey, lebkuchen present an interesting alternative to the darker, molasses-based gingerbreads.

Baking Notes:

The flavor of these cookies improves if you let them sit for a couple of days; however, the icing darkens after a week. To toast nuts, spread them out in an even layer on a rimmed cookie sheet and place in a 350°F oven. Most nuts take about 5–8 minutes to toast. Rotate the pan and shake it halfway through to make sure the nuts toast evenly. Watch their color to make sure they don't burn. For subtle cocoa-spiced cookies, substitute ¹/4 cup of the flour with ¹/4 cup unsweetened cocoa powder.

Recipe:
- ³/4 cup honey
- ³/4 cup dark brown sugar
- ¹/2 cup blanched almonds, toasted
- ¹/2 cup blanched hazelnuts, toasted
- 2 cups all-purpose flour
- ¹/2 teaspoon baking soda
- 1 teaspoon ground cinnamon
- ¹/2 teaspoon ground ginger
- ¹/4 teaspoon ground allspice
- ¹/4 teaspoon ground cloves
- ¹/4 teaspoon ground nutmeg
- ¹/4 teaspoon salt
- 2 eggs
- Finely grated zest of 1 lemon
- 1 teaspoon orange zest
- ¹/2 cup candied citron (lemon and orange peels)

1. Heat honey and brown sugar in a small saucepan over low heat, stirring constantly until the sugar dissolves and the mixture is thin. Remove from heat and cool until just warm, about 10–15 minutes.

2. Using a food processor, finely grind the almonds and hazelnuts with 2 tablespoons of the flour.

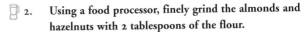

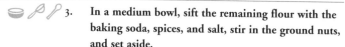

3. In a medium bowl, sift the remaining flour with the baking soda, spices, and salt, stir in the ground nuts, and set aside.

4. In a stand mixer with the whisk attachment, beat the eggs on medium speed for several minutes until light colored and thick. Add the cooled honey mixture and mix until combined.

5. Add the flour mixture and mix with the paddle attachment until combined. The dough will be very stiff, but also very sticky. Add the zests and candied citron and mix just until incorporated.

6. Cover the dough and refrigerate for at least 2 hours, preferably overnight.

7. Preheat the oven to 350°F. Line several cookie sheets with parchment paper.

8. Using a medium (1³/₄-inch) cookie scoop, drop dough onto the cookie sheets about 2 inches apart.

9. Bake for 10–12 minutes, rotating sheets halfway through, until golden. Prepare the glaze(s), below, as cookies bake.

10. Remove cookie sheets from oven and immediately transfer baked cookies to a cookie rack. Use an offset

spatula to spread glaze over the top of each cookie.
Let stand until completely cool and the icing is set,
about 1 hour.

Plain glaze:
1¹/₂ cups confectioners' sugar
1 tablespoon orange or lemon juice
2 tablespoons hot water

Sift confectioners' sugar. Add the juice and water to
make a thick but runny glaze.

Chocolate glaze:
1¹/₂ cups confectioners' sugar
¹/₄ cup cocoa powder
1 tablespoon orange or lemon juice
2–3 tablespoons hot water

Sift confectioners' sugar and cocoa powder. Add the
juice and enough water to make a thick but runny
glaze.

Yield: About 2 dozen cookies

Storage: Store in an airtight container for up to 2 weeks.
These cookies improve with age, so it is best to make
them several days in advance. For softer cookies, put
half an apple in the container for several days.

64a–b. **MADELEINES**

General
Description:
These small French cake cookies are iconic in French cuisine and around the world. It took but a crumb of these beautifully molded golden treats to send the narrator of Marcel Proust's *Remembrance of Things Past* on a meditative journey of memory and identity. They have a delicious, buttery flavor and a light, spongy texture molded into an elegantly fluted seashell shape.

History:
These cookies made their initial debut in the early 1700s in the town of Commercy, in the Lorraine province of France. There are numerous legends surrounding the origin of this cookie's name, including one that suggests they were named after a young woman named Madeleine who first served them to the Duke of Lorraine's son-in-law, King Louis XV.

Serving
Suggestions:

A time-honored tradition in France is dipping madeleines, fresh from the oven, into tea, coffee, or espresso. For Proustian remembrances of things past, serve madeleines with a nice cup of lime flower tisane, an herbal tea.

Baking Notes:
Special madeleine cookie molds are necessary for making madeleines in their iconic form. For more intense flavor, brown the butter instead of just melting it. See **Blondies** for more instructions. Pipe a

thin line of strawberry jam across the center of each madeleine, or dust them with confectioners' sugar.

Recipe:
4 eggs
¹/₂ cup sugar
¹/₄ cup honey
1 teaspoon vanilla extract
1¹/₂ cups all-purpose flour
2 teaspoons baking powder
¹/₄ teaspoon salt
12 tablespoons unsalted butter, melted and cooled

 1. In a stand mixer, combine the eggs, sugar, honey, and vanilla together with the whisk attachment until the mixture is thick and foamy.

 2. Sift the flour, baking powder, and salt over the egg mixture and carefully fold in with a rubber spatula.

 3. Add the melted butter and fold in gently. Cover the batter and refrigerate for at least 8 hours. This will help the madeleines form their distinctive "bump."

 4. Preheat the oven to 400°F. If you don't have a non-stick madeleine tray, butter your trays well. Spoon the batter into each mold about ³/₄ full.

 5. Bake for about 5 to 7 minutes, until the madeleines are golden brown. Cool on a wire rack for a few

minutes, then unmold the cookies and let them finish cooling.

Yield: About 2 dozen madeleines

Storage: Madeleines are best served the same day, but you can store them in an airtight container for up to 2 days. Refresh them by placing in a 300°F oven for a couple of minutes.

65.   **PEANUT BUTTER BLOSSOMS**

General Description: *Peanut butter blossoms are small peanut butter cookies that are pressed down with a chocolate kiss.* Also known as *Black-Eyed Susans,* they are popular throughout the United States and Canada.

History: Peanut butter blossoms are a relatively recent cookie invention. Hershey introduced their Chocolate Kisses in 1907, and **peanut butter cookies** gained popularity in the 1930s. Recipes like this one have been made popular by a number of cookbooks and women's magazines, from *Betty Crocker* to *Better Homes and Gardens.*

Serving Suggestions: Serve peanut butter blossoms with a tall glass of milk, any time of the year.

Baking Notes: Do not use natural peanut butter in these cookies as it is formulated differently and will separate when baking. It is important to wait until the very end of baking to add the chocolate kisses, otherwise they will melt.

Recipe: **Use the same ingredient list as for peanut butter cookies (page 215), plus granulated sugar for rolling and chocolate kisses.**

1. **Follow the recipe for peanut butter cookie dough, adding 2 tablespoons of milk to the dough when you add the egg and vanilla.**

2. **Form tablespoons of dough into balls and roll in sugar. Place on cookie sheets about 2 inches apart.**

3. **Bake for 10 minutes, remove from oven, and place a chocolate kiss in the center of each cookie. Return to the oven and bake for 1 more minute.**

4. **Cool cookie sheets on wire racks for 5 minutes before transferring cookies directly onto wire racks with a metal spatula to finish cooling.**

Yield: Yield: About 3 dozen cookies

Storage: Store in an airtight container for up to 1 week.

66a–b. **PEANUT BUTTER COOKIES**

General
Description:

*The peanut butter cookie is one of the most popular cookies in the United States, second only to the ubiquitous **chocolate chip cookie***. In 1931, the distinctive appearance of the peanut butter cookie was established when Pillsbury published a recipe calling for fork tines to be pressed down on the cookie dough.

History:

Recent discoveries suggest that peanuts were cultivated 10,000 years ago on the slopes of the Andes, where they played an important role in the early empires of pre-Columbian South America. Spanish conquistadors took them across the oceans, and peanuts are now central ingredients in a host of cuisines across the globe. If any one individual can be credited for lifting the peanut to its eminent culinary position, it is the former slave and brilliant polymath George Washington Carver. He urged struggling Southern farmers to plant peanuts because they restored nitrogen to the soil and supplied the protein so badly needed in the diet of impoverished Southerners. Peanut butter was first produced in 1890, and it was advertised as a health food at the 1904 St. Louis World's Fair.

Serving
Suggestions:

Peanut butter cookies can be dressed up with mix-ins like chocolate chips or chopped salted peanuts. In the United States, they are often added to packed lunches.

Baking Notes: Do not use natural peanut butter in these cookies, as it is formulated differently and will separate when baking. If the dough is a little sticky when you are trying to flatten them with the fork, dip the fork in some sugar before pressing down.

Recipe: 1¹/₄ cups all-purpose flour
¹/₂ teaspoon baking soda
¹/₂ teaspoon salt
¹/₂ cup softened unsalted butter
¹/₂ cup light brown sugar
¹/₂ cup sugar
1 egg
¹/₂ teaspoon vanilla extract
1 cup creamy peanut butter

 1. Preheat the oven to 375°F. Grease several cookie sheets or line with parchment paper.

 2. Sift the flour, baking soda, and salt into a bowl and set aside.

 3. In a stand mixer, cream butter and sugars on medium speed for several minutes until light and fluffy. Add the egg and vanilla and mix until combined.

 4. Add the peanut butter and mix until completely combined.

5. Add the flour mixture, and mix on low speed just until combined.

 6. Drop tablespoon-sized balls of dough onto cookie sheets about 3 inches apart. Using a fork, press down on each ball of dough to flatten and create a cross-hatch pattern.

7. Bake for 10 to 12 minutes, rotating sheets halfway through, until golden brown. Cool cookie sheets on wire racks for 5 minutes before transferring cookies directly onto wire racks with a metal spatula to finish cooling.

Yield: About 3 dozen cookies

Storage: Store in an airtight container for up to 1 week.

Variations: **Peanut Butter Chocolate Sandwiches**
Sandwich together two peanut butter cookies with chocolate ganache (using the ganache recipe on page 141) and smooth the edges with a metal spatula.

67. ## PIZZELLES

General
Description: *Pizzelles are thin, wafer-like cookies that have snowflake or floral designs imprinted on them.* The cookies are

made by pouring batter into a pizzelle iron, which has the design cast into it. Pizzelles are usually round and flat, but while they are still warm they can be formed into many shapes. They are often used like French **tuiles** and made into cones or cups for holding ice cream, or kept flat and used to sandwich a sweet filling, like **stroopwafels**. Pizzelles are often flavored with anise seed or anise extract.

History:

Pizzelles are one of the oldest known cookies. The word *pizze* means "round and flat" in Italian, and *pizzelle* is clearly derived from this word. Pizzelles were first made in the Abruzzo region of Italy in the 8th century. Originally, they were made for the Festival of the Snakes, to celebrate Saint Dominica, who supposedly drove away an infestation of snakes in the region. Over time, pizzelles became a popular treat to serve at holidays like Easter and Christmas.

Serving Suggestions:

Pizzelles are beautiful served as they are or dusted with a bit of confectioners' sugar to highlight their design. A multitude of additions complement pizzelles as a topping or sandwich cookie filling: Nutella, jam, or whipped cream. Vary the flavor of the pizzelles by substituting lemon or almond extract for the anise, or adding cocoa powder to make chocolate pizzelles.

Baking Notes:

Today there are home pizzelle irons that resemble

waffle makers or ice cream cone makers. The batter
should be able to drop easily from a spoon onto the
pizzelle iron, but it should not be runny. If your batter seems too thin, add a little flour; if it seems too
thick, add a few drops of water.

Recipe: ²/₃ cup plus ¹/₂ cup all-purpose flour
1¹/₂ teaspoons baking powder
¹/₈ teaspoon salt
2 eggs
¹/₂ cup sugar
2 teaspoons vanilla extract
¹/₂ teaspoon lemon extract
6 tablespoons unsalted butter, melted

 1. Sift flour, baking powder, and salt into a bowl and set
aside.

 2. In a stand mixer with the whisk attachment, whip the
eggs and sugar on high speed until thickened.

 3. Combine the vanilla and lemon extracts with the
melted butter. With mixer running on low speed,
gradually add the butter mixture. Mix just until
combined.

 4. Remove bowl from mixer and add in the flour mixture. Mix with a rubber spatula until the dough is
fully combined and smooth.

5. **Cover batter and allow to rest for 15 minutes.**

 6. **Preheat the electric pizzelle press according to the manufacturer's instructions. Open press and place 2 teaspoonfuls of batter on each pizzelle grid. Bake according to the manufacturer's instructions. Note: the first few pizzelles are never perfect; observe the positioning of the batter and finished color so you can adjust for the following pizzelles.**

7. **Gently lift pizzelles from press and cool completely on a wire rack.**

Yield: About 2 dozen 4-inch cookies

Storage: Store in an airtight container for up to 4 days or freeze stacked in an airtight container layered with waxed or parchment paper for up to 1 week.

---

68. **RED WINE COOKIES**

General Description: *With an alluring aroma of wine and citrus, these cookies are sure to please the hungry and curious alike.* Known as *biscotti al vino* in Italy, this lightly sweet cookie is often made at Christmastime. The cookies are formed into crescents, rings, twists, and a variety of other shapes, and lightly coated in sugar. One version of this recipe has the cookies fried in hot oil and then dipped in honey for a crispy, sticky treat.

History:

Wine has been taken for health reasons since the time of the Romans. Sweet wine digestifs have long served this purpose, presumed to aid in digestion, quell the humors, and cleanse the palate.

Serving Suggestions:

These cookies are popularly baked for Christmas in Italy, and you can make them for the holidays as well. They also make a tasty, sophisticated dessert.

Baking Notes:

This cookie is a good way to use up leftover wine. Although red wine is chosen more often, you can also use white wine, or sweet wines like Marsala. Some versions of this cookie also include a teaspoon of anise seed.

Recipe:

3 cups all-purpose flour
1 teaspoon baking powder
¹/8 teaspoon salt
1 egg
1 cup sugar
1 teaspoon orange zest
¹/2 cup vegetable oil
¹/2 cup red wine
Extra sugar for rolling

1. Preheat oven to 350°F. Line several cookie sheets with parchment paper.

2. Sift flour, baking powder, and salt into a bowl and set aside.

 3. In a stand mixer, beat egg and sugar on medium speed until combined. Add orange zest, oil, and wine, and mix until combined.

 4. Add the flour mixture and mix at low speed until combined.

 5. Form dough into 1-inch balls. Roll each ball into a log and then roll in sugar to coat. Curve the ends of the logs to make a crescent shape. Place cookies on sheets about 1¹/₂ inches apart.

 6. Bake cookies for 18 to 20 minutes, rotating cookie sheets halfway through, until the cookies are golden brown. Cool sheets on wire racks for about 5 minutes before transferring cookies directly onto wire racks with a metal spatula to finish cooling.

Yield: About 3¹/₂ dozen cookies

Storage: Store in an airtight container for up to 1 week.

69. **RUSSIAN TEA CAKES**

General
Description:
This snow-white ball of a cookie is perhaps as well known for its distinctive form as for the astonishing number of names it has garnered around the world. Russian tea cakes are also known as *Mexican wedding cookies, Italian wedding cookies, Swedish tea cakes, snowballs, southern pecan butterballs, Viennese sugar balls,* and *polvorones.* These cookies are quite popular as holiday treats in all their international incarnations—perhaps because of their resemblance to snowballs or the richness of their ingredients.

History:
It is unknown how this cookie recipe acquired so many different names around the world; however, it seems to be a descendant of the first known cookies, the sweet sugar cakes Arabs introduced to medieval Europe. Interestingly, the names *Russian tea cakes* and *Mexican wedding cookies* appear to have originated in the United States in the 1950s.

Serving
Suggestions:

These cookies traditionally make their appearance during the winter holidays, where their snowball-like form is most prevalent, but they are always appropriate for tea time or dessert. This recipe works well with almost any nut; almonds, pecans, hazelnuts, or walnuts are the most popular choices. Spice up the batter by adding 2–3 teaspoons of cinnamon (popular in the Mexican wedding cookie variations) or anise.

Baking Notes: It's important to use fresh, good quality butter and nuts for these cookies as they will strongly affect the flavor of the results. Toasting nuts is always a good way to bring out their flavor and increase their potency in a recipe (see pages 206–7).

Recipe: 2¹/₄ cups all-purpose flour
¹/₄ teaspoon salt
³/₄ cup pecans
¹/₂ cup confectioners' sugar, plus more for rolling
1 cup softened unsalted butter
1 teaspoon vanilla extract

 1. Preheat oven to 350°F. Line two cookie sheets with parchment paper.

 2. Sift flour and salt into a bowl and set aside.

 3. Using a food processor, finely grind pecans with the sugar.

 4. Using a wooden spoon or a stand mixer, beat butter until smooth. Do not whip or overbeat the butter— you do not want to incorporate too much air.

 5. Add the nut mixture and mix to combine. Add vanilla extract and mix to combine. Add flour mixture and

mix just to combine. Do not overmix. Dough will be very crumbly and should not come together.

6. Form 1-inch balls of dough and place on cookie sheet. These cookies do not expand, so they may be placed fairly close together.

7. Bake for 12–14 minutes or until the bottoms are golden and the edges begin to brown, rotating cookie sheets halfway through. Remove cookie sheets from the oven and let cookies cool for 1 minute, then roll each cookie in confectioners' sugar. Once cookies are completely cool, re-roll them in confectioners' sugar.

Yield: About 3½ dozen

Storage: Store in an airtight container for up to 5 days.

70. **SPECULAAS**

General Description: *Speculaas are a spicy Dutch/Belgian cookie traditionally eaten at Sinterklaus, or the feast of St. Nicolas on December 5. They are also known in France as speculoos, and in Germany and Austria as spekulatuis.* The most traditional form of speculaas is a firm, biscuit-like cookie made by pressing the dough into a wooden mold that embosses a decorative pattern on the surface of the cookie, similar to **springerle**. The most common designs for molds are St. Nicolas and windmills; sometimes speculaas are referred to as windmill cookies.

History:

The word *speculaas* is thought to be derived from the Latin word *speculum*, meaning mirror. This possibly refers to the process of forming the cookies, which gives the mirror image of the mold.

Serving Suggestions:

❄ 🎁

Speculaas are a beautiful and impressive cookie to serve at the holidays. The spices traditionally used in the cookies varied from household to household; feel free to find a combination that suits your taste best. Some of the spices often used include cloves, cardamom, cinnamon, anise, white pepper, nutmeg, mace, and ginger.

Baking Notes:

If you cannot find speculaas molds, simply roll out the dough and use cookie cutters to cut out shapes.

Recipe:

¹/₂ **cup blanched almonds, toasted**
1¹/₂ **cups all-purpose flour**
¹/₂ **teaspoon baking soda**
1¹/₂ **teaspoons ground cinnamon**
¹/₂ **teaspoon ground ginger**
¹/₄ **teaspoon ground cardamom**
¹/₄ **teaspoon ground coriander**
¹/₄ **teaspoon ground nutmeg**

^{1}/8 teaspoon ground cloves
^{1}/4 teaspoon salt
^{1}/2 cup softened unsalted butter
^{1}/2 cup light brown sugar
^{1}/2 cup sugar
1 egg

1. Using a food processor, finely grind the almonds with 2 tablespoons of the flour. Whisk together ground almonds with the rest of the flour, baking soda, spices, and salt in a bowl and set aside.

2. In a stand mixer, cream together butter and sugars on medium-high speed until light and fluffy. Add egg and beat until combined.

3. With the mixer on low speed, add in the flour mixture and mix until just moistened and combined.

4. Flatten the dough into a disk, wrap well with plastic wrap, and refrigerate at least three hours, but preferably overnight.

5. Preheat the oven to 350°F. Line several cookie sheets with parchment paper.

6. Roll dough ^{1}/8 inch thick on a lightly floured surface. Cut out cookies and place on sheets about 1 inch apart.

7. **Bake for 10 to 12 minutes, rotating sheets halfway through, until firm and lightly golden around the edges. Cool sheets on wire racks for a couple minutes before transferring cookies directly onto wire racks with a spatula to finish cooling.**

Yield: About 3½ dozen cookies

Storage: Store in an airtight container for up to 2 weeks.

71. **SPRINGERLE**

General Description: *Springerle are among the best-known cookies made by pressing the dough into a carved mold.* There are two ways to form the cookies: with a single carved mold, or with a special carved rolling pin that can emboss an entire sheet of dough at once. The designs range from religious motifs to scenes of everyday life to simple images of flowers and birds. The art of carving springerle molds out of wood is revered. Today, springerle are traditionally made at Christmastime, or for the feast of St. Nicolas in Europe.

History: Springerle originated in the Swabia region of Germany, and the word is said to mean "little knight" or "jumping horse" in German; the term might refer to a popular springerle mold of a jumping horse or the way these cookies rise and spring up in the oven. The use of molds to decorate baked items dates back to ancient Mesopotamia and Egypt; the practice was adopted by the Roman Empire, and Romans used clay or wooden molds to press images onto their cakes. Today, quality molds made during the 15th and 16th centuries, the heyday of molded cookies, are difficult to find; they have become collectors' items.

Serving
Suggestions:
❄ 🎁

Christmastime is the perfect time for these cookies, and they make lovely gifts. The flavor of these cookies actually improves over time, so they can be made in advance.

Baking Notes:
⚠

The traditional leavener for springerle was hartshorn, now known as baker's ammonia, instead of the modern baking soda and baking powder. Note that because the raw cookie dough is left out overnight to dry, these cookies should not be eaten by children, the elderly, or persons with compromised immune systems.

Recipe:

2 eggs at room temperature
1 cup sugar
Zest of 1 lemon, finely grated
1 teaspoon vanilla extract
2 cups plus 3–4 tablespoons all-purpose flour
2 tablespoons whole anise seeds, lightly crushed

1. In a stand mixer with the whisk attachment, whip the eggs on high speed for 2 minutes.

 2. With the mixer running on medium speed, add the sugar in a slow stream.

 3. Once all the sugar is added, whip on high speed until thick and light yellow, about 4 minutes.

 4. Remove the whisk attachment and switch to the paddle attachment; add the lemon zest and vanilla extract, and mix well. With mixer running on low speed, add the 2 cups of flour and mix well.

5. The dough should be smooth and stiff. If it seems sticky, add 3–4 tablespoons of flour as needed. Turn out the dough onto a piece of plastic wrap and flatten to form a $1/2$-inch-thick rectangle.

 6. Wrap up dough and refrigerate for 2 hours. At this point, the dough can be frozen for up to 1 week double wrapped. Defrost overnight in refrigerator.

7. Lightly grease several cookie sheets with butter and sprinkle each sheet with 1 tablespoon of the anise seeds.

8. Take half of the dough from the refrigerator. Roll out on a well-floured surface to $1/4$ inch thick, using

more flour as needed to keep dough from sticking to the board. Using a springerle rolling pin, firmly roll over the dough to imprint the designs.

9. Using a sharp knife or a pizza cutter, cut into cookies using the patterns as guidelines. Transfer cookies to sheets with a spatula, $1/2$ inch apart on top of the anise seeds.

10. Leave cookies out to dry out at room temperature, uncovered, for 12 to 24 hours so that they retain the shape of the imprints.

11. When you are ready to bake the cookies, preheat oven to 250°F.

12. Bake for 40 to 45 minutes or until lightly golden on bottom, rotating cookie sheets halfway through. The tops should remain free of color. The baking time will vary depending on the cookie size—larger cookies can take up to 1 hour.

13. Cool sheets on wire racks for about five minutes before transferring cookies directly onto wire racks with a spatula to finish cooling.

Yield: About 4 dozen $1^3/4$ by $1^1/2$ inch cookies

Storage: Store in an airtight container for up to 3 weeks;

flavor develops over time.

SPRITZ COOKIES

General Description

Spritz cookies, or Spritzgebäck, *are small, buttery cookies made by pushing dough through a device called a* cookie press *or* cookie gun. The cookie press can be fitted with different cutout discs so the dough can be extruded into a variety of shapes, from starbursts to hearts. Although classic spritz cookies are made from a simple butter dough that makes them crisp and golden, many different flavors are also common, including chocolate or marbled. Spritz cookies are made throughout Europe and North America during the holidays, and are often further decorated or iced after baking.

History:

Spritz cookies come from Scandinavia, and their name comes from the German word *spritzen*, meaning *to squirt*. The cookies were made for Christmas celebrations from as early at the 1500s.

Serving Suggestions:

Spritz cookies are fun to dress up for the holidays with various sprinkles and colored icings. The basic cookie dough also works well with other flavored extracts, such as peppermint, lemon, or almond. To make marbled spritz cookies, simply fill half of the cookie press cylinder along its length with plain dough, and then the other half with chocolate dough. They will combine when you press the dough to create a marbled effect.

Baking Notes: The trickiest part of making spritz cookies is getting the dough to the right consistency so that it will dispense easily and retain its piped shape. The dough should be soft and pliable but not too soft. If it does not appear to be dispensing cleanly out of the press, try chilling the dough for 5 to 10 minutes in the refrigerator before trying again. Be sure to hold the cookie press flat against the surface of the cookie sheet so the cookies dispense evenly and cleanly.

Recipe: **2 cups cake flour**
¼ teaspoon salt
¾ cup softened unsalted butter
½ cup sugar
1 egg yolk
½ teaspoon almond extract
½ teaspoon vanilla extract
3 or 4 drops of food coloring (optional)

 1. **Preheat the oven to 350°F. Line several cookie sheets with parchment paper or silicone baking mats.**

 2. **Sift flour into a bowl. Add in the salt and sift again (it is important to sift the flour twice).**

3. In a stand mixer, beat butter on medium speed for several minutes until soft. With the mixer running on low speed, add the sugar in a slow stream and beat until light and fluffy. Add in the egg yolk and both extracts and mix until combined.

 4. Add in the flour mixture and mix until combined. Add a few drops of food coloring if desired.

5. Load the dough into the cookie press per the manufacturer's instructions.

 6. Press cookies onto the cookie sheets about 1^1/2 inches apart. Decorate the cookies with sprinkles, candies, or other decorations. Bake for 8–10 minutes until golden. Cool cookie sheets on wire racks.

Yield: About 5 dozen small cookies

Storage: Store in an airtight container for up to 1 week.

Variation: **Chocolate Spritz Cookies**
Add ^{1}/2 ounce melted chocolate and 2 tablespoons milk to the mixture after adding the egg.

73. **STROOPWAFELS**

General
Description:

The stroopwafel, also known as the syrup waffle cookie, is a Dutch treat made of two thin, round, wafer-like cookies with a sweet caramel filling. The cookies are usually marked with a gridlike imprint, similar to waffles. When the cookies are freshly made, the filling is soft and gooey. If the cookie is bought premade and cooled, the filling is often set to a firm consistency, and it is customary to place the cookie on top of a hot cup of coffee or tea to let the filling soften. In the Netherlands, street markets often have stroopwafel stands with bakers selling the hot, fragrant cookies.

History:

There are records of waffle-making in the Netherlands dating back to the 15th century. Dutch waffles were made in all variations, from thick and soft like modern waffles to thin and crisp, like pizzelles. Inspired by waffles, stroopwafels are a particular specialty that was created in the Gouda region of the Netherlands in 1784. According to legend, a baker created the stroopwafel cookie out of cake crumbs mixed with spices and covered with syrup, then pressed in a mold.

Serving
Suggestions:

Stroopwafels should be served with a cup of hot coffee or tea to soften them and cut the sweetness. Substitute the caramel with a variety of other fillings, such as Nutella, whipped cream, honey, or jam.

Baking Notes: If you cannot find a stroopwafel iron with the tradi-
                 tional waffle markings, a pizzelle iron or waffle cone
                 maker works quite well. Avoid Belgian waffle makers
                 or other irons that have deep indentations.

Recipe: 1¹/₄ cups all-purpose flour
           1 teaspoon baking powder
           ¹/₈ teaspoon salt
           ¹/₂ teaspoon ground cinnamon
           2 eggs
           ³/₄ cup sugar
           1 tablespoon vanilla extract
           6 tablespoons melted unsalted butter
           Caramel sauce or caramel filling

1.   Sift flour, baking powder, salt, and cinnamon into a
      bowl, and set aside.

2.   In a stand mixer with the whisk attachment, whip the
      eggs and sugar on high speed until thickened, about 1
      minute.

3.   Combine the vanilla extract with the melted butter.
      With mixer on low speed, gradually add the butter
      and mix just until combined.

4.   Remove bowl from mixer and mix in the flour mix-

ture with a rubber spatula until fully combined and smooth.

⏳ 5. Cover batter and let it set for 15 minutes.

🔥 6. Preheat the electric iron according to the manufacturer's instructions. Place 2 teaspoonfuls of batter on each grid and press. Bake according to the manufacturer's instructions. Note: The first few are never perfect; observe the positioning of the batter and finished color so you can adjust for the following stroopwafels.

7. Gently lift cookies from press and cool completely on a wire rack.

🗄️⏳ 8. Once cookies are cool, top half of them with 2 teaspoonfuls caramel, and gently sandwich with another cookie. Place sandwiched stroopwafels in the refrigerator for 10 minutes to set the filling.

Yield: 10 sandwich cookies

Storage: Store in an airtight container in the refrigerator for up to 5 days. Store stacked only two-high, layered with waxed or parchment paper.

74. TUILES

General
Description:

Tuiles are very thin, crisp cookies that are typically curved on two sides so they look like roof tiles when presented together, although they come in other shapes. They are pale golden with a dark brown border and have an almost porous appearance. They are often decorated with sliced almonds. They have a light, buttery taste but don't usually have a strong, distinctive flavor; they are traditionally meant to accompany other desserts. Today, however, tuiles are often served by themselves and in more embellished varieties, such as dipped in chocolate or covered with toppings sweet, spicy, or savory.

History:

Tuile means "tile" in French, and the cookie is so named because its curved shape resembles the roof tiles on classic French homes. Tuiles have been a mainstay of French pastry for centuries. When large tuiles are formed into a cup shape for holding fruit and sweet fillings, they are often called tulips. Another popular method for shaping tuiles is by piping the batter into narrow strips; the resulting finger-shaped cookies are called *langues de chat* because they resemble cats' tongues.

Serving
Suggestions:

Tuiles pair very well with soft, creamy desserts like ice cream, soufflés, and rich cakes. Large tuiles make perfect bowls for ice cream sundaes. A plain, curved tuile can be filled with whipped cream and fresh berries. Tuile batter lends itself to endless experimentation; it can be flavored with cocoa powder or ground nuts to create an entirely new cookie.

Baking Notes: For uniformly round tuiles, make a template to use when spreading the batter. One can be easily made by cutting a circle out of a plastic can lid. It will take practice to spread the batter thin enough to bake light and crisp; use an offset spatula to even out the batter. It takes a quick hand to shape tuiles once they come out of the oven. Although it possible to shape them freehand, it's easier to drape the cookie over some sort of form. Roll tuiles around the handle of a wooden spoon to make tightly curled cigarettes, or try molding warm cookies in teacups or muffin tins for cup-shaped tuiles.

Recipe: ¹/₂ **cup softened unsalted butter**
1 cup confectioners' sugar
¹/₂ **teaspoon vanilla extract**
4 egg whites at room temperature
¹/₃ **cup all-purpose flour**

1. **In a stand mixer, cream butter and sugar together on medium speed for several minutes until light and fluffy.**

2. **Add vanilla extract, and add egg whites one at a time,**

making sure each is incorporated before adding the next.

 3. Sift flour over mixture and mix on low until combined.

4. Cover batter and let rest in refrigerator for about 1 hour.

5. When you are ready to bake the cookies, preheat the oven to 350°F. Line several cookie sheets with silicone baking mats.

6. Using a stencil as described in the Baking Notes, spread tablespoons of batter onto the cookie sheets, spacing them about 2 inches apart. Be sure to spread the batter as thinly and evenly as possible: If it is too thick, it will not bake properly. Use a moistened fingertip to smooth the batter out.

7. Bake 8–10 minutes or until the edges turn golden.

8. Cool sheets on wire racks. If you want to shape them, you must do so quickly once they are out of the oven before they harden. If the cookies harden before you can shape them, return them to the oven for 30 seconds to warm and soften them.

Yield: About 2 dozen cookies

Storage: Store in an airtight container for up to 3 days.

75. **TV SNACKS**

General
Description: *TV snacks, or croq-télé, are small, irregularly shaped cookies that are buttery and salty in flavor, meant to be eaten like other salty snack foods.* The pastry chef who created these cookies gave them their name because they seemed like an ideal substitute for chips or other snacks people like to consume in front of the television. TV snacks bake into rich, golden brown, crumbly cookies.

History: TV snacks originated in the bakery of French *pâtissier* Arnaud Larher, who was inspired by the salted butter from his native Brittany. The combination of sweet and salty tastes has long existed in savory cooking, and has slowly made its way to the pastry realm.

Serving
Suggestions: While their name suggests their ideal purpose, the cookies are rich and elegant enough to be served at a party. Packaged into cellophane bags and tied with ribbon, they make lovely gifts.

Baking Notes: TV snacks can also be made with ground hazelnuts. The dough for the TV snacks should be fine and crumbly like coarse meal, but still moist. If you have trouble forming the dough into a cohesive shape, you may want to process the dough a little longer until it sticks together better.

Recipe:

3/4 cup blanched almonds, lightly toasted
1/2 cup sugar
3/8 to 1/2 teaspoon salt, depending on your preference
1 cup all-purpose flour
7 tablespoons cold unsalted butter, cut into 1/2-inch pieces

1. Preheat oven to 325°F. Line several cookie sheets with parchment paper.

2. Using a food processor, grind almonds, sugar, and salt to a fine meal.

3. In a stand mixer, beat flour and cold butter on low speed for a few minutes until mixture has a sandy texture. Add the almond mixture and mix on low speed until the dough starts to form small lumps.

4. Using a small cookie scoop or a teaspoon, scoop a rounded teaspoonful of dough into the palm of your hand and pinch the dough so it sticks together. The cookies can be irregularly shaped. Place them on cookie sheets about 1 inch apart.

5. **Bake for 14 to 16 minutes, rotating sheets halfway through, until light golden brown. Cool sheets on wire racks for about 5 minutes before transferring cookies directly onto wire racks with a spatula to finish cooling.**

Yield: About 2 dozen cookies

Storage: Store in an airtight container for up to 1 week. Or freeze in an airtight container for up to 2 weeks and defrost at room temperature.

---

76. **VIENNESE ALMOND CRESCENTS**

General Description: *Viennese almond crescents are plump, buttery, crescent-shaped cookies dusted with a mixture of confectioners' sugar and vanilla sugar.* They are also known as *vanillekipferl* or *vanillekipferln*, or *Viennese vanilla crescents*. Sometimes they are referred to as *German vanilla crescents*, but the cookies originated in Vienna. They have a rich nutty vanilla flavor and a crumbly, shortbread-like texture. Viennese almond crescents are traditionally made for Christmas in Austria and for Advent in Germany, and they are a staple of Viennese coffeehouses.

History: Viennese almond crescents were invented in Vienna, and spread to Germany. It is possible that their shape came about following the invasion of Austria by the Ottoman Empire. Just as with **rugelach** and croissants, the Austrians showed their defiance by creating foods in the shape of the enemy's symbol and consuming them. The term *kipferln* is used to describe any crescent-shaped pastry in a Viennese bakery.

Serving Suggestions:
❄ 🎁

Although ground almonds are the classic nuts to use in these cookies, they can also be made with ground hazelnuts or walnuts. You can also roll the cookies in confectioners' sugar or vanilla sugar alone, depending on your preference. These cookies are associated with Christmas, which is a perfect time to make them.

Baking Notes:

Vanilla sugar is a useful ingredient to have in the baker's pantry, and is easily made by placing a split vanilla bean in a jar of sugar and letting it sit for about a week. The typical ratio is 1 bean to about 2 cups of sugar. As you use the vanilla-flavored sugar, add new sugar to the jar to replenish the supply. The vanilla bean flavors sugar for a long time.

Recipe:

$^1/_2$ **cup ground almonds**
$^1/_2$ **cup confectioners' sugar**
$^1/_2$ **cup softened unsalted butter**
$1^1/_2$ **teaspoon vanilla extract**
1 **teaspoon almond extract**
1 **cup all-purpose flour**
$^1/_8$ **teaspoon salt**

$^1/_2$ cup vanilla sugar, for coating (See Baking Notes)

1. Sift ground almonds and confectioners' sugar into a bowl and set aside.

2. In a stand mixer, beat butter on medium speed for several minutes until smooth.

3. Add in the almond mixture and mix until combined. Add in the vanilla and almond extracts and mix until combined. Add in the flour and salt and mix on low just until combined and the dough starts clumping together.

4. Turn dough out onto a piece of plastic wrap, wrap tightly, and chill for about 20 minutes.

5. Preheat the oven to 350°F. Line several cookie sheets with parchment paper or silicone baking mats.

6. Form dough into 1-inch balls. Roll into logs and curve the ends to make a crescent shape. Place on cookie sheets about 1$^1/_2$ inches apart.

7. Bake for 8 to 10 minutes, rotating sheets halfway through; the edges of the cookies should turn light brown but the tops should not get too dark. Cool sheets on wire racks for about 4 to 5 minutes. While they are still warm, roll cookies in the vanilla sugar to

coat. Let them finish cooling on wire racks.

Yield: About 2 dozen cookies

Storage: Viennese almond crescents are best enjoyed the day they are made, but you can store them in an airtight container between sheets of wax paper for 2 weeks.

Rolled Cookies

77. **ALFAJORES (CARAMEL SANDWICH COOKIES)**

General
Description:

These classic South American cookies consist of two buttery shortbread-style cookies sandwiching a thick, caramel-like filling. The most common filling is *dulce de leche*, made by cooking milk and sugar together until it caramelizes and achieves a thick pudding consistency. Other common fillings are manjor blanco or jam. *Manjor blanco* is made with ingredients similar to dulce de leche, but the milk and sugar are slowly cooked to prevent it from turning brown. There are many versions of alfajores, and most Latin American countries have their own "official" alfajore; some have the cookie covered in white or dark chocolate, or dusted with confectioners' sugar.

History:

Alfajores originated in the Middle East and traveled with the Moorish invasion of Europe in 711 to Andalusia, Spain, where they took root as a jam-filled cookie rolled in nuts and sugar. *Alfajore* comes from the Arabic word for "stuffed." The cookies then migrated with Spanish explorers to the New World. Alfajores still exist in Spain today, although in a far different form. They are made as a small cake with honey, almonds, and spices, and eaten at Christmastime. In general, the term *alfajores* today usually refers to the South American incarnation.

Serving Suggestions:

Substitute jam or Nutella for the filling, or dip the cookies in chocolate or dust them with confectioners' sugar. Flavor the dough with different spices like cinnamon or anise, or a few teaspoons of citrus zest.

Baking Notes: Although dulce de leche can be made from scratch, one of the easiest ways to make it is with a can of sweetened condensed milk. A traditional method in many Latin American countries is to simply submerse the entire unopened can in a pot of water and let it boil for several hours to cook the milk; however, the can must always remain completely covered in water so it does not explode. A less dangerous method of cooking the condensed milk is described in the recipe below. Alternatively, ready-made dulce de leche is available in specialty groceries.

Recipe:
¹/₂ cup all-purpose flour
1¹/₄ cups cornstarch
1 teaspoon baking powder
¹/₈ teaspoon salt
6 tablespoons softened unsalted butter
¹/₂ cup sugar
1 egg
1 egg yolk
1 teaspoon vanilla extract
Confectioners' sugar for dusting

Filling:

1 can (14 oz) sweetened condensed milk

 1. Sift flour, cornstarch, baking powder, and salt into a bowl and set aside.

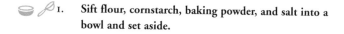 2. In a stand mixer, cream butter and sugar together for several minutes until light and fluffy.

3. Add in the egg and egg yolk and mix until combined. Add in the vanilla extract and mix until combined. Add in flour mixture and mix just until the dough starts to come together.

4. Turn dough out onto a piece of plastic wrap. Flatten into a disk, wrap tightly, and refrigerate for 1 hour until firm.

5. Preheat the oven to 325°F. Line several cookie sheets with parchment paper or silicone baking mats.

6. Roll the dough to 1/4 inch thick on a lightly floured surface.

7. Using a 2-inch fluted cutter, cut out cookies and carefully transfer to the sheets, spacing cookies about 1 inch apart.

8. Chill the sheets for about 15 to 20 minutes until

dough is very firm.

 9. Bake for 8 to 10 minutes, until tops of the cookies are just firm and the bottoms are beginning to color.

 10. Cool sheets on wire racks for 5 minutes before transferring cookies directly onto wire racks with a metal spatula to finish cooling.

 11. **For the filling:** Pour the condensed milk into a metal bowl over a pot of simmering water. Cook over low heat until it becomes thick and dark golden. Stir occasionally to prevent the bottom from burning. It may take a few hours for the condensed milk to cook, but resist turning up the heat too high or the milk could burn. Let the caramel filling cool and thicken before assembling the alfajores.

12. To assemble, sandwich two of the cookies with a teaspoon of the caramel filling. Sift confectioners' sugar over the assembled sandwiches.

Yield: About 3 dozen sandwiches

Storage: Cookies should be served as soon as possible or they will get soggy. Store unfilled cookies in an airtight container for up to 2 days.

78. 📷 **ALGERIAN ALMOND TARTS (DZIRIATE)**

General
Description:
These Algerian tarts combine the delicate aroma of orange flowers with the rich flavor of almonds, glazed with a fine honey-flavored syrup. Known as *dziriat* or *dziriate*, they are popular in Algeria year-round; however, they are particularly prominent at special occasions, such as weddings and the close of Ramadan, when they are served after the sun sets.

History:
The two key ingredients of these cookies—almonds brought by Muslim traders centuries ago and orange flower water—are iconic elements of Maghreb cuisine. These cookies have a strong cultural significance in Algeria and in the Maghreb region, and are often reserved for special occasions.

Serving
Suggestions:
🏵 ☀ ⛄ ❄ ☕
Serve these tarts year-round with tea or coffee. Add a pine nut to the center of each tart for decoration.

Baking Notes:
Rosewater is often substituted with orange flower water, or the two are combined. These tarts are traditionally made with clarified butter, but melted butter also works. Although they are often made free-form, they can be made in tart tins or mini muffin tins.

Recipe:

Pastry:
2 cups all-purpose flour
$^1/_4$ teaspoon salt
$^1/_2$ cup unsalted butter, melted
2 eggs
$^3/_4$ teaspoon vanilla extract
2 tablespoons rosewater or orange flower water
1 teaspoon lemon juice

Filling:
3 cups sliced almonds
$1^1/_2$ cups sugar
2 eggs
$1^1/_2$ teaspoons lemon zest
2 teaspoons rosewater or orange flower water
$^1/_2$ teaspoon vanilla extract

Topping:
$^1/_2$ cup honey
Pine nuts (optional)

 1. Preheat oven to 350°F. Lightly grease a few cookie sheets or line with silicone baking mats.

 2. In a stand mixer, combine the flour and salt. With the mixer running on low speed, gradually add butter, eggs, vanilla, rosewater, and lemon juice. Mix for a few minutes until dough is smooth. Cover dough with a damp cloth and set aside while you make the filling.

3. Using a food processor, grind almonds and sugar to a fine meal. Add eggs, lemon zest, rosewater, and vanilla and process until all ingredients are evenly incorporated.

4. Roll out dough to about $1/16$ inch on a lightly floured surface. Use a 2- to 3-inch cookie cutter to cut out circles from the dough.

5. Drop tablespoonfuls of filling into the center of each circle. Wet fingers with water and pinch the dough together into four corners, forming a cup around the filling. Or, if you have a mini muffin tin or other small molds, fit the dough circles into the molds and fill about $3/4$ full with filling.

6. Place tarts on sheets. Bake for 20 minutes, rotating sheets halfway through until filling begins to brown and the cookies are a light golden color. Remove sheets from oven and place on wire racks. Drizzle honey over each of the tarts. Let tarts cool on sheets before serving.

Yield: About $2^{1}/2$ dozen cookies

Storage: Store in an airtight container for up to 1 week.

79. **ANIMAL CRACKERS**

General
Description:
Many Americans recall with fondness these small cookies shaped in a variety of zoo animals. Often available in stores in small boxes designed to resemble circus train cars, these cookies can also be made at home. Although purists debate whether these are cookies or crackers, the dispute seems primarily semantic.

History:
A variety of cookies called Animals were first imported into America from England in the 19th century. Two of America's larger bakeries united at this time to form the National Biscuit Company, later known as Nabisco. In 1902, they introduced Barnum's Animals in the now familiar boxes, which were designed to be hung on Christmas trees. Often neglected in American cookie books, animal crackers have nonetheless exerted a strong influence on American popular culture. As early as 1928, they were already the namesake of a popular Broadway play, which the Marx Brothers later adapted to film.

Serving
Suggestions:
Animal crackers are perfect snacks year-round. For chocolate frosting, see **Frosted Brownies** on page 141, substituting 2 teaspoons unsalted butter for the cream.

Baking Notes:
Cookie cutters come in a variety of animal shapes, but stencils can be made at home, where the shapes

of these cookies are limited only by the imagination.

Recipe: ¹/₂ cup rolled old-fashioned oats
2 tablespoons light brown sugar
³/₄ cup all-purpose flour
¹/₄ teaspoon baking soda
¹/₄ teaspoon salt
¹/₄ cup softened unsalted butter
2 teaspoons honey
¹/₄ teaspoon vanilla extract
¹/₄ cup cold buttermilk

1. Using a food processor, grind oats until very fine.

2. Combine oats, sugar, flour, baking soda, and salt in a stand mixer, mixing on low speed for about 30 seconds to combine.

3. With the mixer running, add the butter in pieces and combine until mixture is a fine meal.

4. Add honey, vanilla, and buttermilk and mix on low until fully combined.

5. Turn dough out onto a piece of plastic wrap. Flatten into a disk, wrap tightly, and refrigerate for about 1 hour until firm.

6. Preheat oven to 350°F. Line several cookie sheets with

parchment paper.

7. **Roll out dough to about ¹/8 inch thick on a lightly floured surface. Use animal cookie cutters to cut out shapes. Place on cookie sheets about 1 inch apart.**

8. **Bake for 7 to 9 minutes, rotating sheets halfway through. They should turn lightly golden and feel dry and firm to the touch. Cool on wire racks before frosting.**

Storage: Keep in an airtight container for up to 2 weeks, or freeze for several months.

80. **BISCOCHITOS**

General Description: *Biscochitos are crisp, sugary cookies spiced with aniseed and sprinkled with cinnamon sugar.* Sometimes spelled *bizcochitos* or *biscochos*, the word means "little biscuits" or "little cakes" in Spanish. They are also known as *mantecosos*, meaning "buttery ones" in Spain, their country of origin. They are traditionally made with lard but are now usually made with butter or shortening. Biscochito dough is rolled out and cut into shapes, the classic form being a *fleur de lis*. They are known for their flaky lightness, as well as their spicy flavor. Biscochitos are customarily served at Christmastime, often with a glass of wine or a cup of hot chocolate. They were adopted as the state cookie of New Mexico in 1989.

History:

Biscochitos likely descended from Arabic sugar cakes. Spain was introduced to these sugar cakes when the Moors invaded their country in 711. Later, the Spanish explorers of the 16th century brought the cookie to the New World, where it flourished in Mexico.

Serving Suggestions:

Bisochitos are traditionally served at Christmas and other special occasions such as weddings, baptisms, and quinceñeras. They go well with a glass of wine after dinner.

Recipe:

2¹/₂ teaspoons anise seed
1 cup sugar
3 cups all-purpose flour
1¹/₂ teaspoons baking powder
¹/₂ teaspoon salt
¹/₂ cup shortening
¹/₂ cup softened unsalted butter
1 egg
¹/₄ cup brandy or orange juice
¹/₂ cup sugar
¹/₂ teaspoon cinnamon

1. Using a food processor, grind anise seed and sugar until the anise seed is in fine bits.

2. Sift to combine flour, baking powder, and salt in a bowl and set aside.

 3. In a stand mixer, beat anise, sugar, shortening, and butter for several minutes until light and fluffy. Add egg and mix to combine. Add in the brandy or orange juice and mix to combine. Add in the flour mixture and mix to combine.

 4. Turn out dough onto plastic wrap. Flatten into a disk, wrap tightly, and refrigerate for 1 hour until firm.

 5. Preheat the oven to 350°F. Line several cookie sheets with parchment paper or silicone baking mats.

 6. Roll the dough on a lightly floured surface to 1/8 inch thick. Use cookie cutters to cut out shapes. Place cookies on sheets about 1 inch apart.

 7. Combine sugar and cinnamon together in a small bowl. Sprinkle over tops of cookies.

 8. Bake for 8 to 10 minutes, rotating cookie sheets halfway through. Cool cookie sheets on wire racks.

Yield: About 3 dozen cookies

Storage: Cookies should be served as soon as possible or they

will become soggy. You can store them in an airtight
container for up to 2 days.

81a–b. **CHOCOLATE SANDWICH COOKIES**

General
Description:

*The chocolate sandwich cookie, composed of a white,
creamy filling spread between two crisp chocolate wafers,
is one of the most popular styles of sandwich cookie.* The
combination was highly popularized by the creation
of the Oreo cookie by Nabisco. The commercial
process of making Oreos cannot be duplicated in the
home kitchen, but chocolate sandwich cookies in
that style can be easily made. The cookies are usually
made icebox-style by slicing rounds from a log of
dough, or by rolling and cutting out shapes from a
soft dough.

History:

The Oreo cookie was introduced by Nabisco in
1912 as part of a trio of high-end cookie products,
the other cookies being a Mother Goose–themed
biscuit and a crisp British-style biscuit cookie. The
Oreo was the only one to survive the changing tastes
of the American public, and it has so endured in
popularity that it was declared the bestselling cookie
of the 20th century. There is much speculation as to
the origin of the name Oreo; some variously theorize
that it derived from the Greek word *oros*, meaning
hill, as the original cookies were mound shaped, or

from the French word *or* meaning gold, as the packaging for the cookies was originally gold-colored.

Serving Suggestions:

Chocolate sandwich cookies are a classic companion to a glass of cold milk. Crushed sandwich cookies are a delicious topping for ice cream sundaes or cakes. It is simple to vary the filling in the cookies: A teaspoon of peppermint extract in the filling will make these cookies holiday-worthy, or you can experiment with other spreads like lemon curd, Nutella, or peanut butter. If you want an over-the-top presentation, you can dip assembled cookies halfway into melted chocolate for a rich coating.

Baking Notes:

It is best to keep the cookies thin so they bake up light and crisp; if you want them thicker and more substantial, increase the baking time by a few minutes. Make sure the cookies are fully cool before you assemble them so they don't melt the filling. Once the cookies are filled, you should serve them within a few hours or the filling may turn runny and make the cookies soggy.

Recipe:

Filling:
¹/₃ cup softened unsalted butter
1 teaspoon vanilla
¹/₄ teaspoon salt
2 cups confectioners' sugar

1–2 tablespoons milk

Cookies:
1/2 cup sugar
1/4 cup light brown sugar
11/2 cups all-purpose flour
3/4 cup cocoa powder
1/2 teaspoon baking soda
1 teaspoon salt
1 cup softened unsalted butter
1 teaspoon vanilla extract

1. For the filling: In a stand mixer, beat butter, vanilla, and salt together until light and fluffy.

2. With the mixer on low, add the confectioners' sugar slowly. Beat well until fully incorporated. Add the milk a tablespoon at a time until the filling is at a spreadable consistency.

3. Preheat the oven to 350°F. Line several cookie sheets with parchment paper or silicone baking mats.

4. For the cookies: In a stand mixer, mix together the sugars, flour, cocoa powder, baking soda, and salt on low speed just until combined.

5. With the mixer running on low speed, add the butter a few pieces at a time. Mix dough until it resembles

coarse meal.

 6. Turn out dough onto a piece of parchment paper or a silicone baking mat. Roll to about ¹/8 inch thick. If you have trouble rolling out the dough, place another piece of parchment paper or silicone baking mat on top of the dough and roll the dough out between the sheets. Using a 2-inch cookie cutter, cut out rounds and place on the sheets 1 inch apart.

 7. Bake for 12 to 15 minutes, rotating cookie sheets halfway through. Cool sheets on wire racks for about 5 minutes before transferring cookies directly onto wire racks with a spatula to finish cooling.

8. To assemble the cookies, place half of the cookies upside down on a work surface.

 9. Using a small spoon, scoop a small dollop of filling onto the center of each cookie. Top with another cookie right side up. Press the cookies together until the filling spreads out to the edges.

Yield: About 3 dozen cookies (or 18 sandwiches)

Storage: Store unfilled cookies in an airtight container for up to 1 week.

82.   **GINGERBREAD**

General
Description:

Gingerbread is a very old and popular cookie that is associated with Christmas in Europe and America. It comes in two variations: a soft, thick version that is meant for eating, and a thin, crisp version that is often elaborately decorated and used to make Christmas ornaments. All gingerbread has a lightly sweet flavor spiced up with ginger in the dough (so even ornamental gingerbread smells delightful). Gingerbread is cut into all sorts of holiday shapes, and gingerbread people are a popular variety. A stiff, durable version of gingerbread is used for constructing gingerbread houses; sometimes this gingerbread is inedible and hard for structural purposes.

History:

Gingerbread dates to 11th-century Europe. The word was a corruption of the old French word *gingebras* and originally referred to preserved ginger, and not a baked good. Not until the 15th century did it become the common term for the sweet treat. Germany in particular became known for its gingerbread and for elevating it to an art form by popularizing Christmas gingerbread houses. In the 19th century, the tin cookie cutter was developed, allowing gingerbread to be mass produced, and also allowing the general public to make the cookies easily without having to purchase expensive molds.

Serving
Suggestions:
❄ 🎁 🔨

Gingerbread is a classic cookie for holiday decorating. It can be cut into any number of shapes and decorated with icing.

Baking Notes:
⚠

Gingerbread dough needs to be prepared at least 2 days in advance. A baking thermometer is helpful in step 2.

Recipe:

$^1/_2$ **cup plus 2 tablespoons unsalted butter**
$^3/_4$ **cup sugar**
$^1/_2$ **cup light corn syrup**
$^1/_4$ **cup milk**
3 cups bread flour
$1^1/_8$ **teaspoons baking soda**
$3^1/_4$ **teaspoons ground cinnamon**
2 teaspoons ground ginger
$^1/_4$ **teaspoon ground allspice**
3 pinches ground cloves
$^1/_4$ **teaspoon salt**
Icing and colored sugar for decorating (optional)

1. **Line a 9 by 9 inch baking pan with plastic wrap and set aside.**

2. **In a saucepan, melt the butter over medium heat. Add the sugar, corn syrup, and milk. Continue heating the mixture, whisking continuously, until it reaches 100°F. Remove from the heat and set aside.**

3. In a stand mixer, mix together bread flour, baking soda, spices, and salt on low speed.

 4. Add the butter mixture slowly on low speed. Mix a couple minutes more to combine thoroughly.

5. Pour dough into prepared cake pan, cover surface of the dough with plastic wrap, and refrigerate overnight.

6. Two days later, remove the dough from the refrigerator and cut it into 4 pieces. At this point the dough could be double-wrapped in plastic and frozen for up to 2 weeks; to defrost dough, refrigerate overnight.

7. Preheat oven to 350°F. Grease several cookie sheets or line them with parchment paper.

 8. Place one of the chilled pieces of dough on a lightly floured surface and dust with more bread flour. Return other pieces of dough to the refrigerator until you are ready to use them. Roll out the dough to ¼ inch thick. Using cookie cutters, cut out cookies and place on cookie sheets about 1 inch apart.

9. Bake small cookies for 12 to 13 minutes, rotating sheets halfway through, until firm to the touch. (Bake larger pieces 15 to 16 minutes.)

10. Cool sheets on wire racks for a couple minutes before

**transferring cookies directly onto wire racks with a
metal spatula to finish cooling. Decorate cooled
cookies as desired with icing and colored sugars.**

Yield: About 5 dozen small or 3 dozen large cookies

Storage: Store in an airtight container for up to 2 weeks. If
they are decorated, stack them between sheets of wax
paper.

83.  **GREEN TEA COOKIES**

General
Description: *The unique taste of Japanese green tea is perfectly cap-
tured in these distinctive bright green cookies.* Meltingly
tender and not too sweet, they are sophisticated treats.

History: Green tea is a popular form of tea in Asia, especially
in Japan, where it has become intertwined with
Japanese culture. The Japanese learned to grind
dried green tea leaves into a fine powder known as
matcha. Matcha became a central part of the
traditional Japanese tea ceremony, where the bright
green powder is whisked with hot water into a rich
and invigorating tea. This ancient tea has now
moved far beyond the domain of the elegant tea
ceremony and has become quite popular in various
modern desserts—its bitter and intense flavor pairs
well with sugar.

Serving
Suggestions:

Green tea cookies make a beautiful accompaniment for afternoon tea, or as dessert with a glass of white wine or, better yet, sake.

Baking Notes:

Matcha tea comes in a variety of grades; the less expensive grades are much less strong than high-grade matcha, which can get quite pricy. Gauge the amount of powder used in this recipe based on the strength of matcha you purchase.

Recipe:

1¹/₂ cups all purpose flour
¹/₂ cup rice flour
¹/₄ teaspoon salt
2–3 tablespoons matcha powder (3 tablespoons for strong green tea flavor)
1 cup softened unsalted butter
¹/₂ cup sugar
Extra sugar for sprinkling

1. In a bowl, whisk both flours, salt, and matcha powder, and set aside.

2. In a stand mixer, cream together the butter and sugar on medium speed for a few minutes until light and fluffy.

3. Remove bowl from mixer and mix in the flours by hand with a wooden spoon until incorporated.

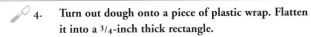

4. **Turn out dough onto a piece of plastic wrap. Flatten it into a 3/4-inch thick rectangle.**

5. **Wrap dough tightly and refrigerate for 2 hours.**

6. **Preheat oven to 325°F. Grease several cookie sheets or line them with parchment paper.**

7. **Place dough on a lightly floured surface and dust with more flour. Gently roll out dough to 1/4 inch thick.**

8. **Use a leaf-shaped cookie cutter or other cutter of your choice to cut out shapes from the dough.**

9. **Place cookies on sheets about 1 inch apart. Sprinkle the tops with sugar.**

10. **Bake for 15 to 17 minutes, rotating cookie sheets halfway through, until edges are lightly golden. Cool sheets on wire racks.**

Yield: About 3 dozen 2 by 1 1/4-inch cookies

Storage: Store in an airtight container for up to two weeks. Double-wrapped in plastic, the dough can be double frozen for up to 2 weeks.

84. **HAMANTASCHEN**

General
Description:

A classic of Jewish baking, these lovely little golden triangles are traditionally filled with a succulent poppy seed or prune filling. Haman was the persecutor of the Jews in the Book of Esther. The word *hamantasch* is thought to have derived from the Yiddish term for "Haman's pockets." Others say that the cookie is named for Haman's tri-cornered hat; in Israel, these cookies are called *oznei haman*, or "Haman's ears." These cookies are an indelible part of the Ashkenazi Jewish cuisine and the holiday of Purim, which commemorates Haman's defeat.

History:

Hamantaschen are associated with the Book of Esther, which recorded the triumph of ancient Persian Jews over a royal aide named Haman. Eastern European Jews developed hamantaschen as part of the Purim holiday tradition of "sending out" small gifts of charity (*mishloach manot*) to friends and those in need. The earliest recorded mentions of the treat date to the 11th century.

Serving
Suggestions:

This traditional gift cookie is perfect for any special occasion. Be sure to include hamantaschen in your Purim holiday gift baskets.

Baking Notes:

Many hamantaschen bakers insist upon the use of poppy seed filling, but apricot, cherry, lemon, or date preserves or prune filling, known as *lekvar*, are also common.

Recipe:
2²/₃ cups all-purpose flour
1³/₄ teaspoons baking powder
¹/₄ teaspoon salt
¹/₂ cup softened unsalted butter or margarine
¹/₂ cup sugar
1¹/₂ teaspoons lemon juice
2 teaspoons finely grated lemon zest
2 eggs
1 teaspoon vanilla extract
2 egg yolks, beaten, for egg wash
Apricot, raspberry, or prune preserves for filling

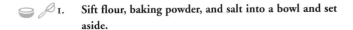

1. Sift flour, baking powder, and salt into a bowl and set aside.

2. In a stand mixer, beat butter, sugar, lemon juice, lemon zest, and eggs together for a couple minutes; the batter should still be slightly lumpy.

3. Add in the flour mixture and mix until combined.

4. Divide the dough into two pieces. Roll out each piece of dough between two sheets of parchment paper about ¹/₈ inch thick.

5. Chill dough (still between sheets of parchment paper)

in refrigerator for 45 minutes until firm.

 6.   Preheat oven to 350°F. Grease several cookie sheets.

 7.   Take one piece of dough from the refrigerator. Using a 2¹/₂-inch cookie cutter, cut out cookies and place on sheets about 2 inches apart.

8.   Drop 2 teaspoonfuls of filling in the center of each circle. Lift one side and firmly pinch each of the two corners. Repeat this two more times, forming a triangular shape.

 9.   In a small bowl, whisk egg yolks. Brush the sides of each hamantasch with the egg wash. Bake 15 minutes or until browned, rotating sheets halfway through the baking time.

Variation: ***Poppyseed Hamantaschen***
For homemade poppyseed filling: Spread 2 cups poppy seeds on a large sheet of wax or parchment paper and work a rolling pin over the seeds until they crack and darken. In a medium saucepan at medium heat, cook poppy seeds with ¹/₂ cup honey, 4 tablespoons corn syrup, and 1 cup water; stirring occasionally, cook for about 10 minutes or until thick. Refrigerate until cool before use.

Yield: About 3 dozen cookies

Storage: The dough for these cookies can be frozen for up to
1 month.

85. **INDIAN ALMOND COOKIES**

General
Description:
*These gorgeous sweet almond diamonds covered with
edible silver are a traditional dessert in India.* Called
badam katli ("almond cookies"), these cookies and a
variation called *kaju katli* ("cashew cookies") are
tremendously popular in Indian communities across
the world. They are traditional fare during the holiday of Diwali, the Festival of Lights when Hindus,
Sikhs, and Jains celebrate the victory of light over
darkness within each of us.

History: India has one of the more ancient culinary traditions
in the world. Almonds were brought to India from
the Middle East with the introduction of Islam to
India and the subsequent Mughal Empire, and were
used as a simple currency by 1583.

Serving
Suggestions:
The ornamental appearance of these cookies suits
them to a host of occasions, such as formal dinners
and weddings.

Baking Notes: These easy, elegant cookies don't even require baking. Silver foil, called *varakh*, *varak*, or *vark* can be
hard to find outside of India, except at Indian gro-

cers. The foil is tasteless, so its omission will only affect the appearance of the cookies.

Recipe: **2 cups blanched almonds**
2 tablespoons milk
1 3/4 cups sugar
1/2 teaspoon cardamom powder (optional)
Silver foil (optional)

1. **In a food processor or blender, grind blanched almonds to a fine powder. Add milk and mix until a smooth paste is acquired.**

2. **In a heavy saucepan, combine the paste, sugar, and cardamom at medium-low heat, constantly stirring to avoid burning; stir 8 minutes or until a lump of dough is formed.**

3. **Turn out the dough onto a lightly greased jelly roll pan or baking dish, flour or grease a rolling pin, and gently roll the dough to approximately 1/4 inch thick. Apply silver foil and press slightly with the foil's paper packaging or a paper towel so that the silver adheres to the dough.**

4. **As the dough cools, its texture resembles that of marzipan. Once it has completely cooled, cut it into 1–2 inch diamond shapes.**

Yield: About 3 dozen cookies

Storage: They will keep up to 1 week if sealed in an airtight
container.

86. **LINZER COOKIES**

General
Description:
*Few cookies are as iconically recognizable or have as ele-
gant a pedigree as the beautiful Linzer cookie.* This
cookie is composed of two crisp, buttery cookies
sandwiching a fruit filling. The top cookie has a
cutout in the center that allows the filling to show
through. Often, the top cookie is sprinkled with
powdered sugar to further the visual contrast.

History: Linzer cookies were developed in the late-1600s in
Austria, where they are known as *Linzer augen*, or
"Linzer eyes." Linzer cookies are an offshoot of the
famous Linzer torte, which was created in Linz,
Austria. The traditional filling for Linzer torte and
Linzer cookies is blackcurrant preserves, although
today redcurrant and raspberry prevail as the fillings
of choice.

Serving
Suggestions:
The elegant and delicate nature of these cookies
makes them a perfect fit for afternoon tea or cocktail
parties. Because of their visual appeal and many decorative shapes, Linzer cookies are a popular treat at

holidays such as Christmas and Valentine's Day, and
they make lovely gifts.

Baking Notes: Although Linzer cookies are traditionally made with
ground almonds, try substituting other nuts—such
as hazelnuts—for a different taste. Roll the dough as
evenly as possible so that all the cookies will be the
same thickness; this will make the assembled sandwiches look better. It is possible to store the rolled
dough in the refrigerator for a few days or in the
freezer for a few months.

Recipe: **1¹/4 cups almonds**
2³/4 cups all-purpose flour
1 teaspoon cinnamon
¹/4 teaspoon ground cloves
¹/4 teaspoon ground cardamom
¹/2 teaspoon baking powder
¹/4 teaspoon salt
1 cup softened unsalted butter
¹/2 cup sugar
1 egg
¹/2 cup raspberry or apricot jam for filling
About ¹/4 cup confectioners' sugar for dusting

 1.   **Using a food processor, finely grind almonds with the
flour.**

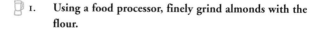 **2.**   **Combine almond mixture with spices, baking powder,**

and salt in a bowl and set aside.

3. In a stand mixer, cream butter and sugar on medium speed for several minutes until light and fluffy.

4. Add egg and mix until combined. Add almond mixture and beat on low until the dough comes together into a ball.

5. Turn out dough onto a clean surface and form it into a flat rectangle about 1 inch thick; wrap in plastic, and refrigerate about 2 hours until firm.

6. Preheat the oven to 350°F. Line several cookie sheets with parchment paper or silicone baking mats.

7. Roll dough to about $^1/16$ inch on a lightly floured surface. Cut out shapes with a 2-inch-wide cookie cutter. Use a small cookie cutter to make cutouts in half of the cookies, so when you make sandwiches the filling will show through. Place cookies on cookie sheets about 1 inch apart.

8. Chill cookies on the cookie sheets for about 15 minutes before baking.

9. Bake 12 to 14 minutes or until the cookies turn golden brown and smell like toasting hazelnuts, rotating cookie sheets halfway through. Cool sheets

on wire racks.

10. **Wait until the cookies are completely cool before assembling them. Stir the jam to soften it, and spread it over half the cookies. Sift confectioners' sugar over the rest of the cookies and place them on top of the jam covered halves.**

Yield: About 3 dozen sandwich cookies

Storage: Let filled sandwich cookies sit for a few hours before serving to let the filling set; however, don't dust them with confectioners' sugar until right before you serve them. Filled sandwich cookies will become soggy after a day. Store unfilled cookies in an airtight container for up to 1 week. Linzer cookies are fairly fragile and need to be stored and transported carefully.

87. **MORAVIAN SPICE COOKIES**

General Description: *These delicate, paper-thin spiced cookies hold the title of "the world's thinnest cookie."* Moravian spice cookies are spicy, crisp wafers baked in large quantities throughout the Christmas season in the southeastern U.S.

History: Members of the Moravian church came to North America as missionaries in the early 1700s, in an effort to reach out to Native Americans and pursue their own religious freedom. They founded the town of Bethlehem, Pennsylvania, in 1741 and in 1766 founded Salem, which became Winston-Salem, North Carolina. Old World recipes for spice cookies have been passed down through many generations.

Serving
Suggestions:
❄ 🎁

Families in the southeastern United States bake these cookies in great quantities during the Christmas holidays, particularly on December 7, the vigil of the Virgin's feast day.

Baking Notes:

It can be tricky to roll the dough so thin. If you are having difficulty, try rolling the dough between two silicone baking mats or two sheets of parchment paper. Another advantage to using this method is that if the dough gets too soft to handle you can easily place the dough between the sheets in the refrigerator for several minutes to let it chill and firm up again.

Recipe:

1¹/₄ cups all-purpose flour
1 teaspoon ground cinnamon
¹/₂ teaspoon ground ginger
¹/₂ teaspoon ground cloves
¹/₄ teaspoon baking soda
¹/₄ teaspoon baking powder
¹/₄ teaspoon salt
¹/₄ cup shortening or softened unsalted butter
¹/₃ cup molasses
¹/₄ cup dark brown sugar

1. Sift together flour, spices, baking soda, baking powder, and salt in a bowl and set aside.

2. In a stand mixer, beat shortening, molasses, and sugar together on medium speed for several minutes until smooth.

3. Add about half the flour mixture and mix on low to combine. Gradually add the rest of the flour mixture and mix until incorporated.

4. Turn out dough onto a piece of plastic wrap. Form into two disks, wrap tightly, and chill in refrigerator for about 1 hour.

5. Preheat the oven to 350°F. Grease several cookie sheets.

6. Roll out one piece of dough at a time on a lightly floured surface to $1/16$ inch thick. Use a 2-inch round cookie cutter to cut out rounds. Place cookies on sheets about 1 inch apart.

7. Bake 8–10 minutes, rotating cookie sheets halfway through. Cookies should be lightly browned at the edges and firm in the center. Cool on wire racks.

Yield: About 5 dozen cookies

Storage:

Store cookies in an airtight container for up to a week. These thin cookies are meant to be baked and eaten in large quantities.

88. **PALMIERS**

General
Description:

Palmiers are striking cookies made with puff pastry dough that is folded and sliced so the cookies bake into a graceful form resembling palm leaves. The cookies are sprinkled with sugar before baking, which gives them a very crisp, flaky texture and rich, caramelized flavor. Palmiers are a mainstay of French bakeries but are also found around the world, sometimes by different names, including *elephant's ears*, *butterflies*, *shoe soles*, or *angel wings*.

History:

Palmiers were invented in the early 1900s in France. The word means "palm tree" in French. Palmiers were created as a way to use up the leftover scraps of puff pastry dough in kitchens. The origins of puff pastry, or *pâte feuilletée*, are uncertain; there are references made to puff pastry, or "puff paste," in cookbooks dating back to the Renaissance.

However, it was the French who perfected the idea of puff pastry, which involved enclosing a block of butter in a flour and water dough, and then folding the dough through multiple "turns." When the puff pastry dough was baked, the moisture between all the layers would expand in the heat, causing the pastry to rise and turn light and flaky.

Serving
Suggestions:

Palmiers are a beautiful cookie to serve for dessert and at parties. You can give them a fancier presentation by sprinkling crushed nuts over the tops of the cookies. Another excellent variation is to add a bit of cinnamon to the sugar for coating the cookies.

Baking Notes:

It is important to keep the puff pastry cool so the butter in the dough does not melt. After you shape the palmiers, be sure to give the dough a good chill in the refrigerator, as this will help the cookies keep their shape. When you are forming the dough, take care not to fold it too tightly or loosely. If it is too loose, the cookies will unfold and lose their shape when baking. If it is too tight, the cookies will not be able to expand properly in the oven.

Recipe:

1 pound frozen puff pastry dough
1 egg, beaten
About 1 cup sugar

 1. **Remove puff pastry from freezer and defrost per instructions on package. The puff pastry should be soft enough to roll, but not too soft or melting. If at any point it seems too soft, place in the refrigerator for about 10 minutes to chill.**

2. Roll puff pastry out on a lightly floured surface to about 18 by 12 by ¹/₄ inch thick. The exact proportions are not critical, but the ¹/₄ inch thick is ideal.

3. Beat the egg with about a teaspoon of water to make an egg wash.

4. Lightly brush egg wash and evenly sprinkle sugar over the surface of the puff pastry.

5. Fold the top long edge down and the bottom long edge up so they almost meet in the middle, leaving a ¹/₂-inch gap, to make a roughly 6¹/₂ by 18 inch rectangle.

6. Brush egg wash and sprinkle sugar over the right 9 inches of the dough.

7. Fold the left side over the right to form a 6¹/₂ by 9 inch rectangle; press down lightly.

8. Use the side of your hand to press down lengthwise on the dough, along the ¹/₂-inch gap you left in step 4. Brush egg wash and sprinkle sugar over the top half (above the ¹/₂-inch gap).

9. Fold the bottom half up over the top half and press down firmly.

10. Wrap dough in plastic wrap and freeze for about 30 minutes to firm before slicing.

 11. When you are ready to bake the cookies, preheat the oven to 375°F. Line a few cookie sheets with parchment paper.

12. Using a sharp chef's knife, slice $^1/_4$-inch-thick strips, starting from the open end (the right hand side of the dough when you were rolling it out). Place on cookie sheets cut side up, about $2^1/_2$ inches apart.

13. Bake for 10 minutes or until the tops start caramelizing and turn golden brown. Remove sheets from oven, flip them over with a spatula, and bake for another 8 to 10 minutes to let the other side caramelize.

14. If you have problems with the palmiers spreading or not caramelizing, try placing a second cookie sheet on top of the cookies when you place them in the oven. Remove the second cookie sheet several minutes before the end to prevent the palmiers from burning.

15. Cool cookie sheets on wire racks for a couple of minutes before transferring palmiers directly onto wire racks with a spatula to finish cooling.

Yield: About 2 dozen cookies

Storage: Store in an airtight container for up to 2 days.
Palmiers will get soggy quickly, so serve them as
soon as possible.

89. **PECAN SANDIES**

General
Description:
*Pecan sandies, also known as pecan shortbread, are an
American version of shortbread made with ground
pecans and brown sugar.* They have the same crumbly,
sandy texture as shortbread, but a sweeter, more
intense caramel flavor. They are usually rolled out or
sliced into rounds and decorated with a pecan half
in the center. Pecan sandies are sometimes confused
with pecan butterballs, which are made with very
similar ingredients but are formed into balls and
rolled in confectioners' sugar.

History: Pecan sandies are an adaptation of Scottish **shortbread** or French **sablé** recipes, using local American
ingredients.

Serving
Suggestions:

Pecan sandies are ideal with afternoon tea. Their
elegant form also makes them perfect for dessert,
either alone or accompanying some ice cream or
cake. If you would like to spice up the flavor of the
cookies, try adding a bit of cinnamon or nutmeg to
the dough.

Baking Notes: As with all shortbread-style cookies, the quality of the butter will determine the excellence of the cookie, so use fresh butter of the best quality you can find. Most importantly, in order to get the best sandy texture, do not overwork the dough; blend the ingredients until they are just combined and stop. If you overmix the dough, you will lose the fine crumbly texture that is the signature of a good pecan sandie.

Recipe: **1¹/₂ cups pecans, toasted**
¹/₃ cup confectioners' sugar
¹/₃ cup light brown sugar
1¹/₂ cups all-purpose flour
¹/₄ teaspoon salt
³/₄ cup plus 2 tablespoons cold unsalted butter
1 egg
¹/₂ teaspoon vanilla extract
About 30 pecan halves for decorating

1. **Using a food processor, finely grind pecans with the sugars.**

2. **Add in the flour and salt and process until combined.**

3. **Cut the butter into small pieces and scatter over the mixture in the food processor. Process until the mixture resembles coarse crumbs.**

4. **Add egg and vanilla and process until the dough**

comes together.

5. Turn dough out onto a piece of parchment paper or silicone baking mat. Roll out to about $1/4$ inch-thickness. Sprinkle the dough with a little flour if it gets too sticky.

6. Cover the dough with plastic wrap and chill in the refrigerator for about 1 hour or until firm.

7. Preheat the oven to 325°F. Line several cookie sheets with parchment paper or silicone baking mats.

8. Using a cookie cutter, cut out cookies from the chilled dough, about 2 inches in diameter. Place a pecan half in the center of each cookie.

9. Bake for 18 to 20 minutes or until the edges of the cookies turn golden brown, rotating cookie sheets halfway through. Cool cookie sheets on wire racks for a couple of minutes before transferring cookies directly onto wire racks with a spatula to finish cooling.

Yield: About 2 to 3 dozen cookies

Storage: Store in an airtight container for up to 1 week.

90a–e. **PINWHEEL COOKIES**

General
Description:

Beautiful and eye-catching, pinwheel cookies stand out on any occasion and can be made in a variety of patterns. Although some of the patterns may seem tricky to make, the dough is a simple vanilla and chocolate cookie. These cookies are a great way to make a variety of eye-catching cookies from one batch of dough.

History:

Gold Medal flour was already including pinwheel cookies in their brand recipes back in 1929. But these cookies have been around as long as bakers have been tinting layers of dough different hues to produce distinctly patterned desserts.

Baking Notes:

The dough can be turned into any pattern imaginable; just slice, roll, and fold the two-toned doughs to create harlequin, bowtie, pinwheel, striped, checkerboard, cross, diamond, or even polka dot cookies.

Recipe:

3 cups all-purpose flour
¹/₂ teaspoon baking powder
¹/₄ teaspoon salt
1 cup softened unsalted butter
1¹/₂ cup sugar
2 eggs
2 teaspoons vanilla extract
2 tablespoons cocoa powder

1. Sift flour, baking powder, and salt into a bowl and set aside.

 2. In a stand mixer, cream butter and sugar at medium speed for several minutes until light and fluffy. Add the eggs and vanilla and mix until combined.

 3. Add the flour mixture and mix on low speed just until combined.

 4. Divide the dough into two parts. Add the cocoa powder to one half and mix to combine.

 5. Form each half into a disk, wrap tightly in plastic wrap, and chill in refrigerator for about 1 hour until firm.

6. Divide each disk into four pieces. Keep one vanilla piece and one chocolate piece out and rewrap and refrigerate the other pieces for later use.

 7. Roll out the chocolate dough about 1/4 inch thick between two sheets of parchment paper. Roll out the vanilla dough the same way, making sure the two doughs are about the same dimensions.

8. Leaving the chocolate dough on top of the parchment, place the vanilla dough on top of the chocolate dough. Run a rolling pin lightly over the doughs to press them together.

9.   Starting with one of the chocolate ends, roll the dough up into a log, using the parchment paper to help.

10. Wrap the log tightly in plastic wrap and chill in the refrigerator overnight. Repeat this process with the other pieces of dough.

11. Preheat the oven to 350°F. Line several cookie sheets with parchment paper or silicone baking mats.

12. Unwrap the log and using a sharp chef's knife, cut slices ¼ inch thick. Place on sheets about 2 inches apart.

13. Bake for 10 to 12 minutes, rotating sheets halfway through, until edges just begin to turn golden. Cool sheets on wire racks for about 5 minutes before transferring cookies directly onto wire racks with a metal spatula to finish cooling.

Yield: About 5 dozen cookies

Storage: Store in an airtight container for up to 1 week.

91. **PISTACHIO ALMOND COOKIES**

General
Description:

These nutty cookies are decorated with green flecks of pistachios and a fan of almond slices. Cookies and sweets made with pistachios are popular in the Middle East; these delicate, buttery cookies will bring a Middle Eastern touch to your dinner parties.

History:

Pistachios were originally cultivated in Western Asia and Persia and have remained an integral part of that region's cuisine. Pistachios were sometimes dyed red to help mask any imperfections on the shells, but this practice is much less common today. It is best not to use any dyed pistachios in cooking.

Serving
Suggestions:

Plate these cookies with a fan of sliced green apples for pretty hors d'oeuvres. They are also excellent palate cleansers alongside coffee, tea, or wine after a meal.

Baking Notes:

To give these cookies even more of a Middle Eastern flavor, add a $^1/_4$ teaspoon cardamom and a teaspoon of rosewater to the dough. When choosing pistachios, pick ones that are already split open, with bright green nuts.

Recipe:

$^1/_4$ **cup pistachios**
$^1/_2$ **cup softened unsalted butter**
$^1/_4$ **cup sugar**

1 teaspoon vanilla extract
1/8 teaspoon salt
1 cup plus 2 tablespoons all-purpose flour
1 egg, beaten, for egg wash
Almond slices for decorating
Extra sugar for decorating

1. Using a food processor, grind pistachios to a fine meal.

2. In a stand mixer, cream butter and sugar on medium speed for several minutes until light and fluffy. Add vanilla, salt, and ground pistachios and mix until combined.

3. Add the flour gradually, and mix on low speed just until combined.

4. Turn out dough onto a piece of plastic wrap, and form into a 1/2-inch-thick disk. Wrap tightly and chill in the refrigerator for about 30 minutes until firm.

5. Preheat the oven to 300°F. Line several cookie sheets with parchment paper.

6. Roll out dough to 1/4 inch thick on a lightly floured surface. Use a round 1³/4-inch cookie cutter to cut out cookies. Place cookies on sheets about 1 inch apart.

7. Brush cookies lightly with egg wash. Place almond

slices on top in a decorative pattern. Sprinkle cookies
lightly with sugar.

 8. Bake for 20 to 24 minutes, rotating sheets halfway
through, until edges are light brown and the centers
are firm. Cool sheets on wire racks.

Yield: About 3 dozen cookies

Storage: Store in an airtight container for up to 1 week.

92a–b. 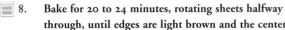 **RUGELACH**

General
Description:

*Rugelach are rich, nutty, crescent-shaped cookies made of
flaky, buttery dough wrapped around a filling of nuts,
dried fruit, and preserves.* This traditional Jewish holiday cookie has been served during the celebration of
Hanukkah for centuries. Rugelach are known by different names in many countries, such as *kipfel* in
Germany and *kifli* in Yugoslavia. In Central Europe,
where the cookies originated, they are made with
sour cream, walnuts, and dried fruit. In America, the
cookies have been adapted with cream cheese in
place of sour cream, and they are sometimes called
cream cheese cookies.

History: *Rugelach* means "little twists" in Yiddish. The tradi- tional curved shape of rugelach mimics the crescent shape of classic croissants, and a common legend is that this form came about as a response to the inva- sion of Austria by the Ottoman Empire in the 1600s. The symbol of the Ottomans was a crescent, and Austrians ate foods in the shape of the enemy's emblem to show their resistance.

Serving Suggestions: Rugelach dough can be filled with a variety of ingre- dients beyond the traditional walnuts and raisins. Many other nuts and fruits, such as pecans, almonds, dried cranberries, and dates are excellent substitutions. Different spreads can be used as well: raspberry jam, honey, or even Nutella. Rugelach are wonderful for holidays and other festive occasions because of their fancy appearance and appealing fla- vor. They go very well with strong coffee.

Baking Notes: The butter and cream cheese for the dough should be at the same temperature and consistency so that they cream together properly and produce the best texture for the dough. If you'd like to increase the flakiness of the baked cookies, sprinkle the rolling surface with a bit of confectioners' sugar. If you find that your cookies are not holding their form during baking, chill the formed cookies for about 10 min- utes before putting them in the oven.

Recipe: **Rolled rugelach:**
¹/₂ cup softened unsalted butter
4 oz cream cheese at room temperature
1 cup all-purpose flour
1¹/₂ teaspoons sugar
¹/₈ teaspoon salt
¹/₂ cup chopped pecans
¹/₄ cup dark or golden raisins
¹/₂ teaspoon cinnamon
¹/₄ cup sugar, plus more for sprinkling
1 egg, for egg wash

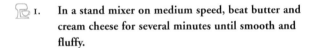 1. In a stand mixer on medium speed, beat butter and cream cheese for several minutes until smooth and fluffy.

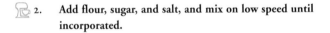 2. Add flour, sugar, and salt, and mix on low speed until incorporated.

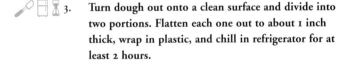 3. Turn dough out onto a clean surface and divide into two portions. Flatten each one out to about 1 inch thick, wrap in plastic, and chill in refrigerator for at least 2 hours.

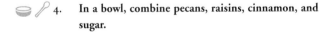 4. In a bowl, combine pecans, raisins, cinnamon, and sugar.

5. Remove one of the portions of dough from refrigerator and roll out on floured surface to a rough

rectangle about 7 by 14 inches.

 6. Cover the dough with the filling, leaving about 1 inch clear on one long side.

7. Roll the rectangle of dough up like a jelly roll, ending with the side that is clear of filling. Press the seam together to seal the roll.

8. Place the roll of dough in the refrigerator, covered in plastic wrap, to chill for about 15 minutes before baking.

9. Meanwhile, preheat the oven to 350°F. Line several cookie sheets with parchment paper or silicone baking mats.

10. Beat the egg with 1 teaspoon of water to make an egg wash. Brush lightly over the top of the roll and sprinkle with sugar.

11. Using a sharp chef's knife, slice the log into 1 inch thick slices and place cut side up on cookie sheets about 1 inch apart.

12. Bake for 16 to 18 minutes, rotating cookie sheets halfway through. The cookies should puff up and turn golden brown. Cool cookie sheets on wire racks before transferring cookies with a metal spatula to

wire racks to continue cooling.

Yield: About 2 dozen cookies

Storage: Store in an airtight container for up to 1 week.

Variation: **Crescent-Shaped Apricot Rugelach**
Replace the pecans, raisins, cinnamon, and sugar with apricot jam.

When you remove the dough from the refrigerator after step 8, roll each one into a circle about 10 inches in diameter. Cover with the filling. Use a pizza cutter or sharp knife to cut the dough into about 16 wedges. Roll each slice up from the bottom and curve the tips slightly to form a crescent shape. Place crescents on cookie sheets, brush with a little egg wash, and sprinkle with sugar before baking as indicated in the recipe.

93.   **SABLÉS**

General Description: *Sablés are classic French butter cookies famed for their simple, clean flavor and delicate, "sandy" texture.* They are similar to shortbread but taste slightly richer due to the eggs in the dough. Excellent sablés are distinguished by their delicate mouthfeel and rich, buttery flavor. Sometimes their edges are sprinkled with colored sugar before baking. Sablés can be eaten individually or sandwiched with a layer of preserves or fruit curd.

History: *Sablé* means "sandy" in French; this refers to the sandy texture of the tender, crumbly cookie. Sablés originated in Normandy, France. Their traditional form was round, with fluted edges and a diamond pattern etched into the top. Today, sablés are made in a variety of flavors and shapes, similar to other French cookies such as **macarons** and **tuiles**.

Serving Suggestions: Although classic sablés are simply flavored with butter, it is easy to add flavorings to the batter. Try a chocolate version by adding a few teaspoons of cocoa powder to the dough in step 4.

Baking Notes: Since butter is the key flavor in sablés, be sure to use the freshest, best quality butter possible. To achieve tender, sandy sablés, it is important not to overwork the dough. When adding the flour, mix only until it looks just incorporated. Resist the urge to turn the speed on high; the more gentle you are with the dough, the better the cookies will be. Chill the dough before baking to help the gluten in the dough relax and help the cookies maintain their round shape in the oven.

Recipe: 1 cup softened unsalted butter
          3/4 cup sugar
          1/2 teaspoon salt
          Zest of 1 lemon
          2 egg yolks at room temperature
          2 cups all-purpose flour
          1 egg white, beaten, for egg wash
          1/4 cup coarse sugar or sanding sugar for decorating

1. In a stand mixer, beat butter on low speed for a few minutes until smooth.

2. Add the sugar, salt, and lemon zest and mix on low speed until combined. Add the egg yolks and mix on low speed until combined.

3. While mixer is on low speed, gradually add the flour and mix until dough is fully combined and smooth.

4. Divide the dough in half and roll each half into an 8 inch by 1 1/2 inch log. Wrap each log in waxed or parchment paper and refrigerate overnight. At this point each log of dough can be double wrapped in plastic wrap and frozen for up to 2 weeks.

5. Preheat oven to 350°F. Grease cookie sheets or line with parchment paper.

6. Remove dough from refrigerator and brush the egg

white on all sides of the log. Sprinkle sanding sugar on the log and roll gently to coat the log evenly and ensure the sugar sticks.

🍪 7. Using a sharp chef's knife, cut the log into $1/2$-inch-thick slices. Place slices on cookie sheets about 1 inch apart.

🔲 🥄 8. Bake for 15 to 17 minutes or until golden brown around edges, rotating cookie sheets halfway through. Cool sheets on wire racks for about 5 minutes before transferring cookies directly onto wire racks with a spatula to finish cooling.

Yield: About $2^{1}/2$ dozen cookies

Storage: Store in an airtight container for up to 1 week.

🍱

94. 📷 **SEA SALT AND WHITE PEPPERCORN COINS**

General Description: *Encrusted with sea salt and infused with the aroma of white peppercorns, these flaky, savory cookies are a dynamic alternative to traditional cookies, crackers, and flat breads.* The large grains of sea salt release their flavor into these crisp cookies in delightful, intense bursts. White pepper is hotter but less aromatic than black pepper, as it contains more piperine (pepper oil) and the outer peppercorn shell has been removed.

History:

In the Middle Ages, salt and pepper became status symbols of fine cookery, but they have been consumed for millennia. Both of these valuable ingredients were traded heavily along early European and Asian trade routes, and even used as a form of currency.

Serving Suggestions:

Serve these savory coins with a hearty bowl of chili or a hot cup of soup. Or plate them with a semi-soft or soft cheese with a creamy flavor (such as Brie or Camembert) with red wine before dinner.

Baking Notes:

Try substituting freshly ground pink peppercorns— or a mixture of white and pink peppercorns. When mixing the dough, do not overwork the butter; it should remain visible in small bits. Kosher salt may be used instead of sea salt, but do not substitute table salt for sea salt; large coarse grains of salt are integral to these cookies.

Recipe:

1¹/₂ cups all-purpose flour
¹/₂ cup cold unsalted butter, cut into ¹/₂-inch pieces
1 teaspoon salt
1¹/₂ teaspoons freshly ground white peppercorns
1 teaspoon lemon zest
1 egg
1 egg white for egg wash
1 tablespoon cracked white peppercorns

1 tablespoon sea salt

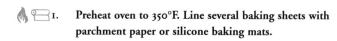

1. **Preheat oven to 350°F. Line several baking sheets with parchment paper or silicone baking mats.**

2. **Using a food processor, combine flour and butter until they form a fine meal.**

3. **Add salt, peppercorns, and lemon zest, and blend briefly to combine.**

4. **Add the egg and blend until the dough starts coming together.**

5. **Roll out dough to ¹/8-inch thick on a lightly floured surface. Using a 1³/4-inch round cookie cutter, cut out cookies and place on sheets about 1¹/2 inches apart.**

6. **Beat the egg white lightly to make an egg wash. Brush cookies with egg wash. Sprinkle some peppercorns and sea salt over the tops.**

7. **Bake for 15 to 18 minutes, until the cookies are lightly golden. Cool sheets on wire racks.**

Yield: About 2 dozen cookies

Storage: Store in an airtight container for up to 1 week.

95a–b. 📷 **SHORTBREAD**

General
Description:

Shortbread is a rich, buttery cookie distinguished by its fine, crumbly texture. Shortbread's distinctive tenderness comes from the high ratio of butter to flour in the dough. Shortbread is typically thick (emphasizing its rich, crumbly texture), flat (due to the lack of leavening), and just barely golden in color. Traditional shortbread from Scotland is made in a large circle that is scored into wedges often called "petticoat tails." Shortbread cookies are commonly found in finger-long rectangles, small rounds, or patterned molds and pricked with a fork in a pattern before baking.

History:

Shortbread is named for its "short" texture: in pastry, *short* describes a tender, crumbly quality. Shortbread originated in Scotland during the medieval period, and also became popular in England. The traditional form of shortbread came from old pagan beliefs; the round shape scored with lines was meant to symbolize the sun, and shortbread was used as an offering at the end of the year.

Serving
Suggestions:

Shortbread is very fine in its classic form, served with a cup of tea or coffee. However, it can be adapted to other flavors, or partially dipped in melted chocolate.

Baking Notes: Texture is paramount in an excellent shortbread, and it depends largely on the quality of the ingredients and the care taken in combining them. Use the best, freshest butter you can find, because its taste will be highlighted in the end product. If you do not have superfine sugar, simply use regular sugar but process it in a food processor for about 45 seconds before step 2. When adding dry ingredients to the butter in step 3, stir only until they are just incorporated. Try to manipulate the dough as little as possible; the less you roll and press it around, the more tender and delicate the results will be.

Recipe: **1¹/₂ cups all-purpose flour**
¹/₂ cup rice flour
1 cup softened unsalted butter
¹/₂ cup sugar
¹/₄ teaspoon salt
³/₄ teaspoon vanilla extract

 1. **Whisk both flours together in a bowl and set aside.**

 2. **In a stand mixer, cream together the butter, sugar, salt, and vanilla on medium speed for a few minutes until light and fluffy.**

 3. **Remove bowl from mixer and mix in the flours by hand with a wooden spoon until incorporated.**

4. Turn out dough onto a piece of plastic wrap and flatten into a 3/4-inch-thick rectangle.

5. Wrap dough with the plastic wrap and refrigerate for 2 hours to firm up. At this point the dough can be double wrapped and frozen for up to 2 weeks.

6. Preheat oven to 325°F. Grease several cookie sheets or line them with parchment paper.

7. Place dough on a lightly floured surface and dust with more flour. Gently roll out dough to 1/4 inch thick.

8. Using a knife or pizza cutter, cut dough into 2-inch by 1 1/4-inch rectangles (or use a fluted rectangle cookie cutter).

9. Place cookies on sheets about 1 inch apart. Prick centers of cookies with the tines of a fork to make a decorative pattern.

10. Bake for 15–17 minutes, rotating cookie sheets halfway through, until edges are lightly golden. Cool sheets on wire racks.

Yield: About 3 dozen cookies

Storage:

Store in an airtight container for up to 2 weeks.

96. **SOUR CREAM BISCUITS (LEPESHKI)**

General
Description:

Almond and sour cream are the two central flavors in these creamy, golden, almond-topped biscuits. Subtly flavored Russian desserts like these cookies often call for sour cream or cottage cheese; in fact, sour cream and dill are the country's most popular condiments.

Serving
Suggestions:

Russian cookies are traditionally served at breakfast with a hot cup of coffee or tea or after dinner.

Baking Notes:

These biscuits use no butter. Yogurt can be substituted for the sour cream, but it yields a heavier cookie. Try substituting almonds with slivers of other nuts, such as macadamias.

Recipe:

2 cups all-purpose flour
¹/₂ cup plus 2 tablespoons sugar
2 teaspoons baking powder
¹/₈ teaspoon salt
1 egg, separated
¹/₂ cup cold sour cream
1 tablespoon milk

$^1/_2$ teaspoon vanilla extract
$^1/_2$ teaspoon almond extract
$^1/_2$ cup sliced almonds for decoration

1. Sift the flour, sugar, baking powder, and salt into a stand mixer bowl.

2. Mix flour mixture on low speed until ingredients are combined.

3. Combine egg yolk, sour cream, milk, and both extracts in a bowl.

4. With the mixer on low speed, add the egg mixture and mix until a soft dough forms.

5. Cover dough and refrigerate for 30 to 45 minutes.

6. Preheat the oven to 400°F. Grease several cookie sheets or line with parchment paper.

7. Roll out dough to $^1/_4$ inch thick on a lightly floured surface. Use a $2^3/_4$-inch round cutter to cut out biscuits. Place cookies on sheets about $1^1/_2$ inches apart.

8. Beat the egg white lightly to make an egg wash. Brush cookies with egg wash. Sprinkle sliced almonds over the tops.

9. **Bake for 8 to 10 minutes, rotating sheets halfway through, until lightly golden brown. Cool cookie sheets on wire racks.**

Yield: About 2 dozen cookies

Storage: Store in an airtight container for up to 3 days.

97. **SOUTH AFRICAN SPICED WINE COOKIES (SOETKOEKIES)**

General Description: *Also known as* soetkoekies *("sweet cookies" or "sweet biscuits"), these treats hail from South Africa and its "Cape Dutch" cookery tradition.* A unique combination of local African, Dutch, English, and Indian cuisines comes together to create this memorable cookie.

History: In South Africa, summer is in full stride for the Christmas holidays, so these cookies are often brought in cookie tins to the beach for holiday celebrations. Europeans had already visited the region as early as 1487, but it was the Dutch East India Company and Dutch colonizers who brought cookies to South Africa in the 1600s.

Serving Suggestions: These cookies are perfect for picnics and trips to the beach. They pair well with hot coffee, tea, or wine.

Baking Notes: Carefully measure the spices and the wine. For a stronger wine flavor, increase the amount of wine by as much as $1/4$ cup; be aware that a few tablespoons of additional flour will be needed to maintain a workable dough that can be rolled. Muscatel or Madeira wines can replace the port or sherry.

Recipe:
2 cups all-purpose flour
$1/2$ teaspoon baking soda
$1/2$ teaspoon cream of tartar
2 teaspoons ground cinnamon
$1^1/2$ teaspoons ground nutmeg
$1^1/2$ teaspoons ground cloves
$1/8$ teaspoon salt
1 cup light brown sugar
$3/4$ cup chopped almonds
$1/2$ cup cold unsalted butter, cut into $1/2$-inch pieces
2 eggs
$1/4$ cup red wine, port, or sherry
1 egg white, beaten, for glaze

 1. **Sift flour, baking soda, cream of tartar, spices, and salt together into a stand mixer bowl.**

 2. **Add the sugar and chopped almonds and mix with paddle attachment to combine.**

 3. **Add the butter and combine for a few minutes on medium until the mixture resembles coarse crumbs.**

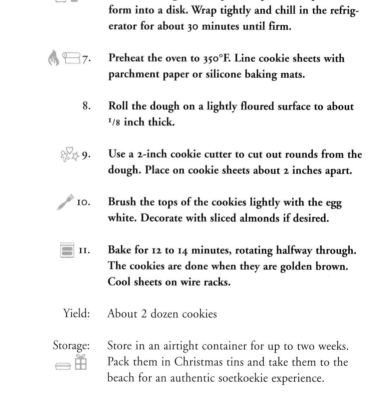

4. Add eggs one at a time and beat until incorporated.

5. Add red wine and mix to combine.

6. Turn out dough onto a piece of plastic wrap, and form into a disk. Wrap tightly and chill in the refrigerator for about 30 minutes until firm.

7. Preheat the oven to 350°F. Line cookie sheets with parchment paper or silicone baking mats.

8. Roll the dough on a lightly floured surface to about 1/8 inch thick.

9. Use a 2-inch cookie cutter to cut out rounds from the dough. Place on cookie sheets about 2 inches apart.

10. Brush the tops of the cookies lightly with the egg white. Decorate with sliced almonds if desired.

11. Bake for 12 to 14 minutes, rotating halfway through. The cookies are done when they are golden brown. Cool sheets on wire racks.

Yield: About 2 dozen cookies

Storage: Store in an airtight container for up to two weeks. Pack them in Christmas tins and take them to the beach for an authentic soetkoekie experience.

98. 📷 **STAINED GLASS COOKIES**

General
Description:

These elegant, transparent cookies make twinkling holi-day decorations. Stained glass cookies are often trimmed with ribbon and hung from Christmas trees like **gingerbread cookies**.

History:

Stained glass cookies have been a Christmas favorite since the 1950s. They are traditionally Christmas cookies, but they can be served as pretty, decorative cookies for any special celebration.

Serving
Suggestions:

These cookies make a gorgeous holiday display. Stud the rolled-out cookies with sprinkles or sanding sugar for added sparkle. To hang them as Christmas tree decorations, poke 1 hole through each cookie with a drinking straw in step 5; once the baked cookies are cool, loop ribbon through the hole.

Baking Notes:
⚠️

Not surprisingly, stained glass cookies are very fragile when hot, so handle with care.

Recipe:

3/4 cup softened unsalted butter
1 cup sugar
1 egg
2 1/2 cups flour
1/4 teaspoon salt
1 teaspoon vanilla extract
Various colors of hard candy

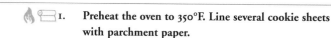

1. Preheat the oven to 350°F. Line several cookie sheets with parchment paper.

2. In a stand mixer, cream butter and sugar at medium speed until light and fluffy.

3. Add the egg and mix until combined.

4. Add flour, salt, and vanilla, and mix until combined.

5. On a lightly floured work surface, roll the dough $1/4$-inch thick. Use variously sized cookie cutters to cut cookie shapes and then cut smaller "windows" into those shapes. Transfer to the cookie sheet about 1 inch apart.

6. Crush candy in separate sealed plastic bags with a rolling pin or meat mallet, then fill the cookie windows with crushed candy.

7. Bake for 8–10 minutes or until the edges start to turn golden, rotating cookie sheets halfway through. Let cookie sheets cool on wire racks for a few minutes before gently removing cookies with a metal spatula to continue cooling.

Yield: About 4 dozen cookies

Storage: Store stained glass cookies in an airtight container
for 1 week.

---

99. **SUGAR COOKIES**
See also Sugar Cookies (drop), pages 111–13.

Recipe: 1²/₃ cups all-purpose flour
¹/₂ teaspoon baking powder
¹/₄ teaspoon salt
¹/₂ cup softened unsalted butter
³/₄ cup plus 2 tablespoons sugar
1 egg at room temperature, beaten
1 teaspoon vanilla extract
Royal icing (recipe follows) and colored sugars if
decorating

 1. Sift together flour, baking powder, and salt in a bowl
and set aside.

 2. In stand mixer, cream together the butter and sugar
on medium speed for several minutes until light and
fluffy.

 3. With mixer on low speed, gradually add the egg and
vanilla and mix until well combined. Add the flour
mixture gradually. Mix until fully incorporated and
the dough is smooth and uniform.

4. Divide dough into 2 pieces and flatten into ¹/₂-inch-thick discs.

5. Wrap dough and refrigerate for 2 hours. At this point the dough can be double wrapped and frozen for up to 2 weeks.

6. When you are ready to bake the cookies, preheat oven to 325°F. Grease several cookie sheets or line them with parchment paper.

7. Place dough on a lightly floured surface and dust with more flour. Gently roll the dough ¹/₈-inch thick.

8. Using a cookie cutter, cut out cookies and place on sheets about 1 inch apart.

9. Bake for 14–16 minutes, rotating sheets halfway through, until edges are golden brown. Transfer cookies to wire racks with a metal spatula to cool.

10. Once cookies are cooled, decorate them with icing and colored sugars.

Royal Icing:
2 egg whites
1 tablespoon lemon juice
3 cups powdered sugar
Food coloring in desired colors

I. **Using a mixer with the whisk attachment, combine all the ingredients and whisk for several minutes on high speed until the mixture is thick and shiny opaque white. It should have the consistency of glue. If it is too thin, add more powdered sugar by teaspoonfuls as needed. If it is too thick, add water by teaspoonfuls as needed.**

 2. **Divide icing into bowls for coloring. Keep the bowls covered or the icing will dry and harden. Add food color to icing to achieve desired hues.**

Yield: About 3 dozen 2$^{1}/_{2}$ inch cookies

Storage: Store in an airtight container for up to 10 days. If they are decorated, stack them between sheets of wax paper.

---

100. **SWEDISH SANDWICH COOKIES (SYLTKAKOR)**

General Description: *These popular Swedish cookies are a staple throughout Scandinavia.* The cookies alone, topped with chopped almonds, are known as *mörkakors*, and are themselves quite popular; with jam-filled *syltkakor*, the acidity and sweetness of fruit jam combine with the buttery almond richness of the cookie to create a truly mouth-watering delight.

History: The star is a central symbol in Scandinavian Christmas celebrations, and star-shaped syltkakor are a common treat at these festivities. In Sweden, sandwich cookies are usually filled with the strong, tart flavors of currant, raspberry, or cherry jam.

Serving Suggestions: These cookies are classic cookie tin stuffers; separate layers of cookies with wax paper. These cookies can be served unfilled; in that case, this recipe would make double the yield.

Baking Notes: Substitute almonds with finely chopped pecans or macadamia nuts. Use star-shaped cookie cutters for traditional Swedish sandwich cookies.

Recipe: **1¹/₄ cups all-purpose flour**
¹/₈ teaspoon salt
¹/₂ cup softened unsalted butter
¹/₄ cup plus 2 tablespoons sugar
1 egg yolk
¹/₂ teaspoon almond extract

Topping:
1 egg white
2 tablespoons sliced almonds, finely chopped
1 tablespoon sugar

Filling:
$^1/_2$ **cup jam or preserves**

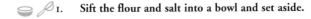 1. Sift the flour and salt into a bowl and set aside.

2. In a stand mixer, cream butter and sugar on medium speed for several minutes until light and fluffy. Add the egg yolk and almond extract and mix until combined.

3. Add the flour mixture, and mix on low speed just until combined.

4. Cover dough and refrigerate for 30 minutes.

5. Preheat the oven to 350°F. Line several cookie sheets with parchment paper.

6. Roll out dough to $^1/_8$ inch thick on a lightly floured surface. Use a $2^1/_2$-inch round or star-shaped cutter to cut out cookies. Use a smaller $^3/_4$- to 1-inch round or star-shaped cutter to make cutouts in half of the cookies, so when you make sandwiches the filling will show through. Place cookies on sheets about $1^1/_2$ inches apart.

7. Beat the egg white lightly to make an egg wash. Brush the cookies that will become the sandwich tops with the egg wash. Sprinkle with the chopped

almonds and sugar.

 8. Bake for 10 to 12 minutes, rotating sheets halfway through, until the edges are light golden. Cool cookie sheets on wire racks.

9. Wait until the cookies are completely cool before assembling them. Stir the jam to soften it, and spread it over half the cookies, then top with the other half to make sandwiches.

Yield: About 2 dozen sandwich cookies

Storage: Store unfilled cookies in an airtight container for up to 1 week.

Table of Equivalencies

Volume

U.S.	Metric
1/4 teaspoon	1.25 milliliters
1/2 teaspoon	2.5 milliliters
1 teaspoon	5 milliliters
1 tablespoon (3 teaspoons)	15 milliliters
1 fluid oz (2 tablespoons)	30 milliliters
1/4 cup	60 milliliters
1/3 cup	80 milliliters
1/2 cup	120 milliliters
1 cup	240 milliliters
1 pint (2 cups)	480 milliliters
1 quart (2 pints)	960 milliliters
1 gallon (4 quarts)	3.84 liters

Weight

U.S.	Metric
1 oz	28 grams
4 oz (¹/4 lb)	113 grams
8 oz (¹/2 lb)	227 grams
12 oz (³/4 lb)	340 grams
16 oz (1 lb)	454 grams

Formulas

Cups to liters	Multiply cups by 0.236
Cups to milliliters	Multiply cups by 236.59
Inches to centimeters	Multiply inches by 2.54
Ounces to grams	Multiply ounces by 28.35
Ounces to milliliters	Multiply ounces by 29.57
Tablespoons to milliliters	Multiply tablespoons by 14.79
Teaspoons to milliliters	Multiply teaspoons by 4.93

Oven Temperatures

Degrees Fahrenheit	Degrees Centigrade	British Gas Marks
200°F	93°C	—
250°F	120°C	1/4
275°F	140°C	1
300°F	150°C	2
325°F	165°C	3
350°F	175°C	4
375°F	190°C	5
400°F	200°C	6
450°F	230°C	8
500°F	260°C	10

High Altitude Baking

Feet above sea level	Per teaspoon baking powder	Per cup sugar	Per cup liquid
3,000	-1/8 teaspoon	-1/2 to 1 tablespoon	1 to 2 tablespoons
5,000	-1/8 to 1/4 teaspoon	-1/2 to 2 tablespoons	2 to 4 tablespoons
7,000+	-1/4 teaspoon	-1 to 3 tablespoons	3 to 4 tablespoons

Common Conversions

All-purpose flour

1 tablespoon	$1/4$ oz	7 grams
1 cup	5 oz	140 grams

Granulated sugar

1 tablespoon	$1/2$ oz	14 grams
1 cup	5 oz	140 grams

Brown sugar

1 tablespoon	$1/2$ oz	14 grams
1 cup	8 oz	220 grams

Confectioners' sugar

1 tablespoon	$1/4$ oz	7 grams
1 cup	4 oz	110 grams

Butter

1 tablespoon		$1/2$ oz		14 grams
1 cup	16 tablespoons	8 oz	2 sticks butter

Milk or heavy cream

1 cup	8 fluid oz

Further Reading

Baggett, Nancy. *The All-American Cookie Book*. New York: Houghton Mifflin, 2001.

Bloom, Carole. *The International Dictionary of Desserts, Pastries, and Confections*. New York: Hearst Books, 1995.

Borghese, Anita. *The International Cookie Jar Cookbook*. New York: Charles Scribner's Sons, 1975.

Cook's Illustrated Magazine, ed. *Baking Illustrated*. Brookline, Massachusetts: America's Test Kitchen, 2004.

Daley, Regan. *In the Sweet Kitchen*. New York: Artisan Books, 2001.

Gand, Gale. *Butter Sugar Flour Eggs*. New York: Clarkson Potter, 1999.

Greenspan, Dorie. *Baking: From My Home to Yours*. New York: Houghton Mifflin, 2006.

Greenspan, Dorie. *Paris Sweets*. New York: Broadway Books, 2002.

Medrich, Alice. *Bittersweet: Recipes and Tales from a Life in Chocolate*. New York: Artisan, 2003.

Montagne, Prosper, ed. *Larousse Gastronomique*. New York: Clarkson Potter, 2001.

Pappas, Lou Seibert. *Christmas Cookie Book*. San Francisco: Chronicle Books, 2000.

Rodgers, Rick. *Kaffehaus*. New York: Clarkson Potter, 2002.

Walter, Carole. *Great Cookies*. New York: Clarkson Potter, 2003.

Yard, Sherry. *The Secrets of Baking*. New York: Houghton Mifflin, 2003.

Zuckerman, Kate. *The Sweet Life*. New York: Bulfinch Press, 2006.

Index

Numbers in **bold** (for example, **77**) are photograph numbers, and can be used to locate cookies in the photograph section. All other numbers are page numbers.

Acknowledgments

A huge thank you to Caroline Romanski, whose pastry expertise and generosity were invaluable in creating the recipes for this book. This book would not have been possible without her. Thank you also to Robyn Beechuk and Renee Ting, recipe developers and testers extraordinaire.

Additional thanks to: Monica Glass for contributing recipes for lebkuchen, speculaas, and pfeffernüsse, and being a great hostess for my research trip to New York; the inspirational Dorie Greenspan and Arnaud Larher for allowing me to include an adaptation of their TV Snacks in this book; Jane Dimmel for generously sharing her mother's recipe for spritz cookies; Lizz Souders for sharing her recipe for orange delight cookies; the rest of the Quirk staff who pitched in and helped bake cookies for the photoshoot; Steve Legato for making my cookies look better than I could have imagined, and for patiently allowing a photography neophyte to watch and ask endless questions during the photoshoot; Margaret McGuire for her patience, resourcefulness, and guidance, not to mention awesome editing and baking skills; Michael Rogalski for his fantastic design work, done in a seemingly impossible amount of time; Mindy Brown and Quirk for giving me the opportunity to create this book; all the readers of my website Dessert First; and my parents and sisters for their love, and for encouraging me to follow my dreams.

And to Mike, for his boundless love and support through all the months of my filling the kitchen with dirty bowls and mixers, subjecting him to taste-tests of "just one more batch" of cookies, and endlessly obsessing over the text. Thanks for always being there, and for being a great cook so I didn't have to live on just cookies while writing this book.